MINECRAFTERS

MORE THAN 2000 HILARIOUS JOKES AND RIDDLES ABOUT BOOBY TRAPS, CREEPERS, MOBS, SKELETONS, AND MORE!

MICHELE C. HOLLOW, JORDON P. HOLLOW,
STEVEN M. HOLLOW, AND BRIAN BOONE

Illustrations by Amanda Brack

Sky Pony Press
New York

Sky Pony Press books may be purchased in bulk at special discounts for sales promotion, corporate gifts, fund-raising, or educational purposes. Special editions can also be created to specifications. For details, contact the Special Sales Department, Sky Pony Press, 307 West 36th Street, 11th Floor, New York, NY 10018 or info@skyhorsepublishing.com.

Sky Pony® is a registered trademark of Skyhorse Publishing, Inc.®, a Delaware corporation.

Visit our website at www.skyponypress.com.

10 9 8 7 6 5 4 3 2 1

Library of Congress Cataloging-in-Publication Data is available on file.

Cover design by Brian Peterson
Cover illustration credit: Hollan Publishing, Inc.
Cover and interior illustrations by Amanda Brack

Print ISBN: 978-1-5107-4733-3
Ebook ISBN: 978-1-5107-4744-9

Printed in the United States of America

Portions of this book were previously published as *Jokes for Minecrafters* (ISBN: 978-1-5107-0633-0), *Hilarious Jokes for Minecrafters* (ISBN: 978-1-5107-0632-3), and *Uproarious Riddles for Minecrafters* (ISBN: 978-1-5107-2717-5)

CONTENTS

JOKES FOR MINECRAFTERS

HILARIOUS JOKES FOR MINECRAFTERS

UPROARIOUS RIDDLES FOR MINECRAFTERS

JOKES FOR MINECRAFTERS

INTRODUCTION

A joke book about Minecraft can be called niche (or very specific) humor. We, however, are calling it *Notch* humor. If you know Minecraft, you may have groaned or giggled, and you certainly will get that joke. We have found a secret language of sorts that is just shared by you—the fans of the game.

Kids in the gaming world call Minecraft a phenomenon. Your parents may call it an obsession. Fans—you know who you are—keep on coming back because Minecraft nurtures your creativity. It makes perfect sense to compare it to time spent playing in a sandbox or maybe even the original LEGO bricks—the ones before the kits, when nothing held you back. Markus Persson, the creator of the game, once said the only limit in Minecraft is your imagination.

In addition to letting your imagination run wild, Minecraft allows you and your fellow players share a sense of humor. While blowing things up, causing fires, and other forms of destruction may sound ominous in most situations, in Minecraft, these things are sheer fun.

So, in between running from and fighting hostile mobs and trading with villagers, enjoy these jokes, riddles, puns, limericks, poems, tongue twisters, haikus, and trivia facts about your favorite game.

CHAPTER 1

BOOBY TRAPS AND BOMBS

JOKES

Q: Where did the creeper go after the explosion?

A: Everywhere!

■

Q: What did the player say when he blew up the creeper?

A: "Dynamite!"

■

Q: Why do creepers like Rice Krispies?

A: Because they go *snap, crackle, POP!*

■

Q: What goes "Sneak, sneak, sss! Kaboom!"?

A: A creeper with a bomb in his hands!

Q: What do you get when you cross a creeper with a bomb?

A: A bomb that sneaks up on you!

■

Q: Why don't they have knock-knock jokes in Minecraft?

A: Because hostile mobs don't knock on your door. They blow it up!

Q: How did Steve feel after he stepped on a landmine?

A: He felt *de-feeted.*

Q: What is a Minecraft player's favorite TV show?
A: *The Big Bang Theory!*

■

Q: What do you get if you cross a creeper with a monkey?
A: A ba-BOOM!

■

Q: What did the player say on his way to a creeper rock concert?
A: "I hope I don't get blown away!"

■

Q: How do you make a creeper shower?
A: Give him a hand grenade!

■

Q: What movie do Minecraft players like to watch?
A: *The Terminator.*

■

Q: What do you call a cow that eats a bomb?
A: Udder destruction!

Q: What would you get if a famous French emperor stepped on a landmine?

A: Napoleon Blownapart!

■

Q: What did the player say after falling into a booby trap?

A: "That was a blast!"

Q: What do you call a creeper with a bomb in his hands?

A: It doesn't matter; he will be blown to smithereens!

First player: “What you don’t know won’t hurt you.”
Second player: “Tell that to the player who just landed on a booby trap!”

■

First Player: “Did you hear about the player who covered a lot of territory?”
Second Player: “No. How’d that happen?”
First Player: “He stepped on a booby trap and is all over the place!”

■

First player: “Building landmines is an expensive hobby.”
Second player: “Why?”
First player: “It can cost an arm and a leg!”

■

First player: “I never wanted to follow in Steve’s footsteps.”
Second player: “Why?”
First player: “Because he stepped on a landmine!”

■

First player: “So far, I’ve bombed ten creepers!”
Second player: “Sounds like you’re having a blast tonight!”

First player: "What happens if you swallow uranium?"
Second player: "You get *atomic ache*."

■

First player: "Did you see all of the Minecraft merchandise in the stores and online?"
Second player: "Yes, it's a booming industry!"

■

First player: "Did you hear about the book that fell on the player's head?"
Second player: "How did it happen?"
First player: "He only had his-*shelf* to blame!"

■

First player: "How is Minecraft different from LEGO?"
Second player: "LEGO doesn't have bombs or booby traps!"

■

First player: "Did you hear about the player who thought the creeper was giving out free hugs?"
Second player: "No, what happened?"
First player: "He went *KABOOM*!"

Q: How fun was the Minecraft party?

A: It was a blast!

■

First player: "Did you hear about the player who built a fireplace inside his TNT house?"

Second player: "No."

First player: "Really? He was all over town."

First player: "Did you hear about the player who heated his house with lava?"
Second player: "Was he burned to a crisp?"
First player: "No, he just went with the flow."

■

First player: "I just saw a new player destroy a thousand creepers."
Second player: "Wow! That sounds amazing."
First player: "It was good, but I wasn't blown away!"

■

Knock, knock.
Who's there?
Hand grenade.
Hand grenade who?
Kaboom!

TONGUE TWISTERS

Brad borrowed Betty's bombs.

Bobby blasted big black bats.

Bombs being built by Billy.

Terry targets tyrants with TNT.

Cam creams creepy creepers crawling 'cross the carpet.

Clever Carole caught creepers—*kaboom*!

Before bombs burst, back off!

Betty borrowed Bonnie's big bomb!

MINECRAFT LIMERICKS, POEMS, AND HAIKUS

There once was a player named Jay.
He was having a very bad day.
A mob of creepers attacked.
They just wouldn't stay back.
And sad Jay was all blown away!

■

A blaze swooped in with fireballs blazing.
Some cows nearby were grazing.
The blaze was caught in a trap,
He most surely did snap,
And the explosion was quite amazing.

■

While being pursued on a beach,
The player created a breach.
He threw his last bomb
And escaped without harm,
From the creeper, he was now out of reach.

■

A player tried to retreat.
The situation looked like defeat.
A nearby big ghast
Shot fireballs that blast
And hit him on his very big feet.

■

As explosions lit up the night,
Bombs burst with all of their might.
A zombie, quite young,
Stuck out his tongue
And dared me to come over and fight.

■

I threw a bomb from way up high.
It fell from the dark night sky.
Mobs of ghasts were down below.
Hitting them, I waved hello.
One escaped with a great big sigh.

■

The bomb I made was first class.
No other could ever surpass.
Armed with such power,
I vowed I would shower
A creeper that was giving me sass.

■

A bold player on a new mission
Had untested bombs in his munitions.
Would they be sound?
Would creepers hit the ground?
Yeah, his plan came to fruition!

■

Watch where you travel.
Beware, don't step on gravel.
It's a booby trap!

■

Beware, be careful.
Booby traps are hidden here,
And there, and there, too!

■

Did you hear that sound?
Oh no, a ticking time bomb!
Last sound was *kaboom*!

■

A zombie chased me from the start.
He almost captured my beating heart.
A booby trap I laid
Was the price he had paid.
Now, he's in many body parts!

■

A legendary player named Pap
Hit targets while taking a nap.
Such precision and ease,
Mobs he could tease
And trick them with hidden booby traps!

■

A mob of zombies hid down by the creek.
For our hero, the world looked bleak.
Hostile mobs kept on forming,
Strange creatures were swarming.
Poor hero ran out of bombs last week.

■

This battle was not what I planned.
I had to attack the zombie by hand.
Behind him I crept,
And I could have wept,
Because my bomb fell into the sand!

■

There once was a player named Nero.
He wanted to feel like a hero.
He bombed a hostile mob
And made this his job.
His chances were greater than zero!

■

He built a booby trap kit
And waited for mobs to steal it.
For in it was a bomb.
Outside it seemed quite calm.
Opened, the mob would get hit.

■

The bomb the player built was a brute.
He disguised it to look rather cute.
His trap he did set
While making a bet
That the creeper would explode en route!

■

A player with a big smile
Built a bomb projectile.
If stepped on just right,
The enemy would take flight
And would explode in great style!

■

A player planned all through daylight
Of the creepers he would bomb in the night.
Large numbers gathered and grew,
Soon there would be just a few.
In blasting them he took great delight!

■

I launched a giant bomber.
This creeper would be a goner.
He fought with great might—
A terrible fight.
He lost, and now I'm much calmer!

■

There once was a player named Tom.
He got hold of a very large bomb.
It blew up in his face.
He was flung into space.
Now, that's the end of poor Tom.

RIDDLES, PUNS, AND MINECRAFT PHRASES

I take just four seconds to explode. What am I?
TNT!

I can scare creepers and I'm not TNT. What am I?
A cat!

Puns about Minecraft mishaps can be classified as *a leg gory.*

Landmines. Where do you stand on them?

As I stood on a landmine, I thought, *My feet are killing me!*

If everything in Minecraft is square, how do you get a *round* of ammo?

Hey, I wonder if this could be one of those booby . . .
Kaboom!

CHAPTER 2

BOO-BOOS MADE BY NOOBS

TONGUE TWISTERS

Noobs know Nether, not nexus.

No, not never know Nether.

Noobs Nancy, Ned, and Nathan needed Nether wart.

Patty poorly poured potions.

Sheila saw six sheep sleeping.

Steve's sword sliced squid.

Ghasts got Gary grounded.

MINECRAFT LIMERICKS, POEMS, AND HAIKUS

Think back and recall
The first time you played Minecraft.
We can see you smile!

■

There once was a noob named Chuck.
He completely ran out of luck.
He tripped over his cat
And fell into a vat.
Now he is covered in muck.

■

There once was a noob named Paul.
He fought a creeper and gave it his all.
He escaped from a cave
By digging sideways
Then triggered a massive rock fall.

■

There once was a noob named Clive
Who escaped by taking a nosedive!
He landed in a vat.
His body went splat!
Ah, poor Clive is no longer alive!

■

A noob crept out onto the field.
He hid behind a sheep as he kneeled.
A ghast took direct aim.
The dim noob was slain.
For a sheep makes a terrible shield.

A new player that wasn't so brave
Hid deep, deep in a cave.
His bright torch—a mistake—
Caused spiders to wake.
He retreated and gave them a wave.

■

Take this wise advice:
Jump in and play without fear.
You will have much fun!

■

A noob was crossing the street,
Searching for villagers to meet.
Instead, he confronted a ghast.
He tried to run past,
But was caught and suffered defeat!

■

The noob started out quite well.
Players rallied around and would yell:
"Hurray for the noob that defeats all the mobs!"
With potions, converted them to gooey globs,
Which he slipped on, tumbled, and fell!

■

There once was a noob named Bob.
He successfully slaughtered a mob.
He fell into a hole,
Was impaled on a pole.
Now Bob's a human kebab!

■

There once was a noob named Sam.
In the water he went and swam.
A zombie nearby
Caught his twinkling eye
And is eating Sam like a ham.

■

An unwise noob laid in waiting.
A creeper, he was baiting.
Soon spotted was he,
Crouching down by a tree.
Now his life is quickly fading!

■

There once was a noob named Ned.
He didn't use his head.
Bringing water into the Nether
Wasn't very clever.
Being so thirsty, he fled.

■

A noob passed through a portal.
It almost made him feel immortal.
He defeated a ghast
And had the last laugh
And made this noob snort and chortle.

■

A noob as strong as an ox
Loved playing with Minecraft blocks.
He created a village,
Which a creeper did pillage.
His world was reduced to just rocks.

■

There once was a noob named Bob.
He spotted his very first mob.
He thought they looked cute.
Instead they were brutes
Who made griefing him their job.

■

Please don't blame the noob.
You were one some time ago.
We learn from mistakes.

■

Noobs always improve.
If they try and don't give up
They just get better.

■

If success is far
And just feels beyond your reach,
Just keep on trying!

■

There once was a noob named Nancy.
Playing Minecraft was her fancy.
With gusto, she burrowed straight down.
Broke her pickaxe, which caused her to frown.
Now Nancy's agitated and antsy.

■

Think noobs know nothing?
They will try and try again
And have lots of fun!

DID YOU HEAR . . . ?

Did you hear about the noob who looked an Enderman right in the eyes?
He searched the site for sunglasses!

Did you hear about the noob who built a fire in her wooden house?
The entire house went up in flames!

Did you hear about the noob who spent days trying to get his minecart to move and finally realized he had to power the rails?
He went nowhere!

Did you hear about the player who thought he was too powerful to need armor or swords?
What a noob!

Did you hear about the noob who thought the pool of lava was gold?
He respawned to tell the tale!

Did you hear about the noob who touched a cactus?
He's all scratched up!

Did you hear about the noob who tried to hypnotize an Enderman?
He was destroyed.

Did you hear about the noob whose favorite block is air?
Nothing happened!

Did you hear about the noob who thought a bed of lava was a hot tub?
It destroyed him!

Did you hear about the noob who put on armor but forgot her sword?
It ended poorly!

Did you hear about the noob who hugged a creeper?
He went boom!

Did you hear about the noob who punched a tree?
Her fists are full of splinters!

Did you hear about the noob who tossed meat to a creeper?
No one's seen him since!

Did you hear about the noob who mistook lava for a pool of water?
He sure learned his lesson!

Did you hear about the noob who climbed a tree to escape a ghast?
Unfortunately, he didn't see the other mobs hiding in that tree!

Did you hear about the noob who spent hours mining obsidian with a wood pick?
He was board to death!

Did you hear about the noob who built a dirt house with no torches?
In seconds it was filled with skeletons!

Did you hear about the noob who learned the hard way that you can't kill a ghast with a sword?
She was destroyed!

Did you hear about the noob who made a monster trap in Peaceful mode?
She didn't know why monsters didn't spawn!

Did you hear about the noob who went out exploring and forgot where her home was?
She is still looking!

Did you hear about the noob who kept on calling the health icon a heart?
She tried to draw smiley faces on the screen, too!

Did you hear about the noob who spent hours pressing the arrow key in order to move?
He went nowhere!

Did you hear about the noob who changed the words to Taio Cruz's song "Dynamite" so that it mentions Minecraft?
Her popularity has exploded all over the Internet.

Did you hear about the noob who shot an arrow into the air?
He missed!

Did you hear about the noob who tested TNT in her house?
She rocked the roof!

Did you hear about the noob who built a hotel in the Nether?
His guests thought his beds were a real blast!

Did you hear about the noob who kept on bugging her friend to share recipes?
She now makes a tasty spider stew!

Did you hear about the noob who actually invited a creeper into his house because he didn't know what it was?
His house blew up!

Did you hear about the noob who was running so fast that he didn't see the edge of the cliff?
He respawned!

Did you hear about the player who was so freaked out that when she was attacked by a few mobs she forgot to use her sword?
What a noob.

Did you hear about the noob who worked so hard to gather gold, only to drop it when he was chased into a ravine to escape hostile mobs?
He is still searching for it.

Did you hear about the noob who tried to mine stones with a hoe?
All the other players laughed, "Ho, ho, ho."

Did you hear about the noob who spent fifteen hours trying to craft a saddle?
I don't know wither or not she ever finished!

Did you hear about the noob who forgot to turn on the sound?
He couldn't hear the creeper. . . .

Did you hear about the noob who thought the Enderman looked friendly?
He was destroyed!

Did you hear about the noob who spent the entire day gathering wood and didn't craft it into wooden planks?
He got board!

Did you hear about the noob who tried to sleep in a bed in the Nether?
She had one of those dreams where you're falling right after you get blown up!

Did you hear about the noob who tried to mine a diamond with a gold pickaxe?
He's still at it!

Did you hear about the noob who forgot and turned off Peaceful mode after he placed torches all through the tunnel?
The creepers saw the light!

Did you hear about the noob who tried to dig up and hit gravel?
It was a rocky situation.

Did you hear about the noob who spent hours trying to make a torch out of a flint?
He's steel trying!

Did you hear about the noob who stood on the TNT when it went off?
It was a moving experience!

Did you hear about the noob who burned leaves too close to his house?
He was left with nothing.

Did you hear about the player who left the door open and then creepers came to visit!
What a noob.

Did you hear about the noob who was so excited to build his wooden house next to the lava?
He was all fired up.

Did you hear about the noob who tried to build a bridge with sand?
He sunk!

Did you hear about the noob who built a house with only one exit?
No, but the hostile mobs did!

Did you hear about the noob who caught on fire and tried to put the flames out with a bucket of water?
Unfortunately, it was a bucket of lava!

Did you hear about the noob who mistook a zombie for a player?
He was lunch!

Did you hear about the noob who wanted to build a popular club and thought TNT was a decorative block?
It really exploded!

Did you hear about the noob who didn't know how to land in Survival mode?
He's still soaring!

Did you hear about the noob who crafted bows backward?
He became the target!

Did you hear about the noob who didn't know how to move water around?
He placed buckets all around and waited for it to rain!

Did you hear about the noob who threw a damage potion at a zombie?
Nothing happened!

Did you hear about the noob who tried to break gold blocks with his right hand?
Now they call him Lefty.

Did you meet the noob who was too afraid to venture outside even though her home was in Peaceful mode?
Of course not!

Did you hear about the noob who spent the first few minutes of nightfall running around without any weapons?
It wasn't long before she was destroyed.

Did you hear about the noob who didn't store her valuables and weapons in a chest at her base?
She was dis-armed!

Did you hear about the player who ventured into the Nether without armor or weapons?
What a noob!

Did you hear about the noob who ran into her house to hide from a creeper?
Creepers are very good at hide-and-get-blown-up!

Did you hear about the noob who thought creepers were passive mobs?
Wrong, oh so wrong!

Did you hear about the noob who built a house in a cave and forgot to build a fourth wall?
She had unexpected company!

Did you hear about the noob who didn't know he was on multiplayer and mistook a friend for a creeper?
That will teach his friend to just drop in!

Did you hear about the noob who traded diamonds for gold?
Ooh, shiny!

Did you hear about the noob who didn't pack food during the cave exploration?
It didn't end well for him!

Did you hear about the noob who built her house high up on gravel?
Everything went downhill!

Did you hear about the noob who repeatedly fell into the same lava pool five times?
She respawned over and over and over and over and over again!

Did you hear about the player who trapped himself?
What a noob!

Did you hear about the noob who built a house with an iron door that locked from the outside?
He's still inside!

Did you hear about the noob who left TNT near redstone?
Kaboom!

Did you hear about the noob who thought zombies and skeletons could survive daylight?
He hid inside his house all day!

Did you hear about the noob who decided to make a lava moat around his wooden castle?
It was flaming!

Did you hear about the noob who fought creepers with a wooden shovel?
She thought that was her strongest weapon!

Did you hear about the player who built his house in Creative mode and spotted creepers?
He hid! What a noob.

Did you hear about the noob who saw a shovel and started thinking about digging a mine in her own backyard?
Her family has a lovely new swimming pool!

Did you hear about the player who tried making tools out of redstone, lapis, and sandstone?
What a noob!

Did you hear about the noob who decided to decorate her bedroom with creeper traps?
She caught her little brother on Monday and her mom on Tuesday and was grounded for the weekend!

Did you hear about the noob who wore obsidian?
She's incredibly hot!

Did you hear about the noob who put his mom's diamond ring on the end of a stick and tried to dig with it?
He was grounded for a week.

Did you hear about the noob who visited a farm?
She ran away from the pigs because she thought they might attack her!

YOU MIGHT BE A NOOB . . .

You might be a noob if you think those hissing voices are coming from an Ender Dragon.

You might be a noob if you spot a creeper and go outside your house.

You might be a noob if you build a dirt house.

You might be a noob if you pet a wolf.

You might be a noob if you mistake redstone for rubies.

CHAPTER 3

LAVA, DROWNING, AND OTHER DASTARDLY WAYS TO DIE

JOKES

Q: How are cacti like creepers?

A: You can't hug either of them!

■

Q: Why was the player shocked?

A: Because he was struck by lightning!

■

Q: When is it okay to make jokes about dying by volcano?

A: When the dust settles.

Q: What did one player say to his girlfriend who fell into a volcano?

A: "I *lava* you!"

Q: What pool is bad for swimming?

A: A lava pool!

■

Q: What did the creeper say when he saw the volcano explode?

A: "Hsss, what a *lavaly* day!"

Q: Who's a volcano's favorite singer?
A: Johnny Ash!

■

Q: Why did the creeper and the ghast blast each other?
A: They had a falling out!

■

Q: What did the player call an adorable volcano?
A: *Lavable!*

■

Q: Why couldn't the hippie be saved from drowning?
A: He was too far out.

■

Q: What did the player say right after the volcano exploded?
A: "Unbe*lava*ble!"

■

Q: What did the player say right before he fell into a pool of lava?
A: "I'm going to go with the flow!"

First player: "What was the funniest time you were destroyed in Minecraft?"
Second player: "I was fleeing from a creeper and ran into another creeper!"

■

First player: "Can you recall the funniest way you were destroyed?"
Second player: "Water pushed me into lava!"

■

First player: "I'll always remember my friend's last word."
Second player: "What was it?"
First player: "Creeper!"

■

First player: "You know the saying, *He that fights and runs away, lives to fight another day*?"
Second player: "Yes, but in Minecraft, if you stay, fight, and die, you can always respawn!"

First player: "Did you hear about the player who ran straight into a cactus?"
Second player: "No, what happened?"
First player: "He's on pins and needles!"

■

First player: "Did you hear about the player who was shocked while taking a selfie playing Minecraft?"
Second player: "Yes, but on the bright side, selfie sticks are also lightening rods!"

■

First player: "My cactus died!"
Second player: "Man, you are less nurturing than the desert!"

■

Q: Why did the player throw the chicken into the fire?
A: He wanted it barbecued.

TONGUE TWISTERS

David digs deep down and drowns!

Felicia and Francis fall furiously fast.

Falling Floyd flipped.

Digging diamonds, Dan drowned.

MINECRAFT LIMERICKS, POEMS, AND HAIKUS

There once was a player named Matt.
A stinky ghast pushed him into a vat.
Instead he caught a whiff,
Stumbled, and fell off a cliff.
Now, poor Matt went splat.

■

Roaring quite loudly,
Lava spilled every which way.
Now it is quiet.

■

Glittery diamonds
Sparkle in boiling lava.
Oops, I am drowning.

■

Diving in lava
Is never recommended
To retrieve diamonds.

■

The creeper was near.
I ran and fell off a cliff,
To avoid creepers!

■

So much disruption.
The volcano's eruption
And interruptions!

■

There once was a player named Jane.
Many gamers thought she was insane.
It was diamonds she spotted.
Oh, how she plotted.
Diving in lava caused her much pain.

■

There once was a player named Paul.
He killed nine creepers one fall.
Nine's an excellent score,
Yet all he wanted was more!
But he lost, 'cause you can't win them all!

■

High up in the air he did sniff,
A rotting zombie—eww, what a whiff!
He felt sick to his stomach
And wanted to plummet,
So he jumped off a very big cliff.

■

There once was a player named Marie.
She ran from a creeper and scraped a knee.
He pushed her in lava.
She hit him with a guava.
She's lucky because she broke free!

RIDDLES, PUNS, AND MINECRAFT PHRASES

If one synchronized swimmer drowns in Minecraft, do the others drown, too?

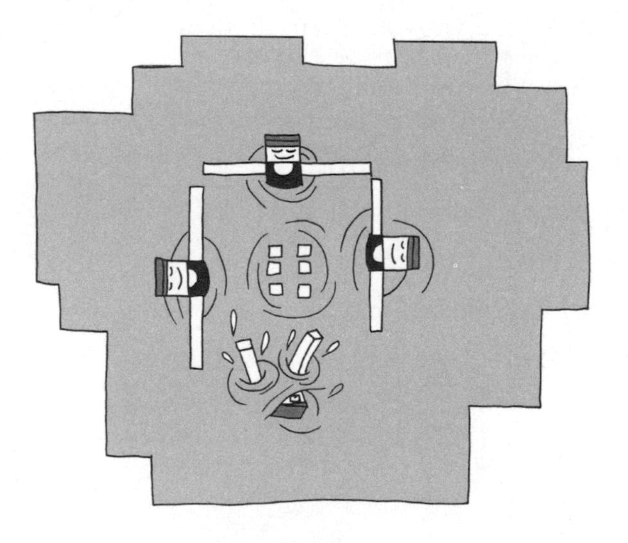

As long as I feed, I live. But when I drink, I die. What am I?
Fire.

I am used to transport lava. What am I?
A bucket.

I am evil. I start numerous forest fires. What am I?
Lava!

What did the volcano say to the two players having a conversation?
"I didn't mean to *inter-erupt*!"

DID YOU HEAR . . . ?

Did you hear about the player who tripped while carrying a bucket of lava?
He was destroyed!

Did you hear about the player who accidentally shot himself with an arrow?
He was thankful that he could respawn!

Did you hear about the player who trapped himself in a wall?
He now knows to add doors.

Did you hear about the player who built a floor made of lava?
She's now hot-blooded!

Did you hear about the player who made a horde of ghasts upset?
There were a lot of tears shed!

Did you hear about the player who greeted an Enderman with a warm embrace?
She'll never make that mistake again!

Did you hear about the player who tried to irritate a bunch of slimes?
She's still trying to wash them off of her, but her skin is really smooth!

Did you hear about the creeper who didn't cross the road?
He was about to cross the road, then saw a player and exploded!

Did you hear about the player who tried to make an Ender Dragon a pet?
It was a noble attempt.

Did you hear about the player who asked the Enderman to be his best friend?
He decided he was better off on his own!

Did you hear about the player who rode a pig into a void?
We haven't heard from him since!

Did you hear about the player who dug straight down?
He didn't make it.

Did you hear about the player who built a beautiful home while it was freezing outside?
He made a lovely ice sculpture.

Did you hear about the player who told the witch her house was destroyed?
In turn, she destroyed him!

Did you hear about the player who blew himself up with TNT?
I'm sure you can guess what happened!

Did you hear about the player who thought he could fly in Survival mode?
He couldn't!

Did you hear about the player who walked in on two creepers?
He was destroyed!

Did you hear about the player who tried to farm in the Nether?
He was destroyed!

Did you hear about the player who tried to put a saddle on a creeper?
He went boom!

Did you hear about the player who was pushed into a ravine when water fell on him?
He made a big splash!

Did you hear about the player who was pushed off a cliff by a skeleton?
He respawned and told me about it!

Did you hear about the player who met a super creeper?
He was super destroyed!

Did you hear about the player who is out of this world?
He fell into a void!

Did you hear about the player who let a creeper style her hair?
She had a brush with death!

Did you hear about the player who kept a creeper as a pet?
He went boom.

Did you hear about the player who gorged himself on rotten meat?
He had a tummy ache!

Did you hear about the player who swam with squid?
He's eating calamari!

Did you hear about the player at the pool?
He was yelling that he needed a lifesaver and the lifeguard asked, "Sure, what flavor?"

Did you know that if you jump off a twenty-four-block tower you can survive falling twenty-three blocks?
It's the twenty-fourth block that can hurt you!

Did you hear about the player who was swept up in tornado mod?
He was blown away!

CHAPTER 4

THE OVERWORLD

JOKES

Q: Why couldn't the Ender Dragon enter the Overworld?

A: Because he was past the portal of no return!

Q: Why are charged creepers always up-to-date?

A: Because they keep *current*!

Q: How do you know a dead charged creeper from a pile of healthy ones?

A: It's got no spark!

■

Q: What do charged creepers call a power failure?

A: A current event!

■

Q: How do charged creepers know when they fall in love?

A: They can feel the spark.

■

Q: What's gray and crispy and hangs from a tree?

A: An amateur charged creeper!

■

Q: What happened to the player who touched a charged creeper?

A: He got shocked!

■

Q: What did the zombie say when he ate a charged creeper?

A: "Shocking!"

Q: What would you call slimes that nibble on charged creepers?
A: *Electro-maggots.*

■

Q What do you call someone who touches a charged creeper?
A: Electrocuted!

■

Q: What hostile mob often winds up in jail?
A: Charged creepers!

■

Q: What's black and jumps up and down in a forest fire?
A: A burned player.

■

Q: What did the pig say in the desert?
A: "I'm *bacon* out here."

■

Q: If you are lost in the desert, is it better to ask for directions from villagers living in NPC villages or from snow golems?
A: Villagers, because snow golems in the desert are a mirage.

Q: Why didn't the player starve in the desert?

A: Because of all of the sand-*witches* there!

■

Q: What's a witch's favorite ballet?

A: *Swamp Lake.*

■

Q: Why did Steve go across the ocean?

A: To get to the other tide!

■

Q: What did the player say to the guardian when he was fleeing from the ocean?

A: "Sea ya later!"

■

Q: What did the ocean say to the shore?

A: Nothing, because oceans can't talk!

Q: What did the player get from the creeper who was struck by lightning?

A: A charge!

■

Q: What did the player say to the guardian?

A: "Let's not be *anemones*!"

■

Q: What washes up on tiny beaches?

A: Microwaves!

■

Q: Why did the cactus cross the road?

A: He was stuck to Steve!

Q: Why was the cactus sad?

A: No one would hug him!

■

Q: Why was the cactus messy?

A: A creeper exploded when it hugged it!

■

Q: Why was the player prickly?

A: He hugged a cactus.

■

Q: Why did the wolf point to the player when it saw a killer bunny?

A: He knew killer bunnies only attack wolves if players aren't around!

■

Q: How did the player thwart the killer bunny?

A: He named it Toast!

■

Q: Why is it hard to tell Minecraft witches apart?

A: Because you never know which witch is which!

Q: Why don't Minecraft witches fly on broomsticks?
A: They are afraid of flying off the handle!

■

Q: What is a witch's favorite subject in school?
A: Spelling.

■

Q: Why did the player put name tags on the witches?
A: So he could tell which witch was which!

■

Q: What do witches eat?
A: Creepypasta!

■

Q: What noise does a witch's breakfast cereal make?
A: Snap, cackle, pop!

■

Q: What's a cold evil candle in Sweden called?
A: The wicked wick of the North!

Q: What did the player say to the witch he was battling?

A: "With any luck, you'll soon be well and get up for a spell."

■

Q: What's more dangerous than one angry witch?

A: Two angry witches!

■

Q: Why is a witch like a candle?

A: They're both wick-ed!

■

Q: What do you get when you put a witch in an icy biome?

A: A cold spell!

■

Q: What is a witch's favorite saying?

A: "We came, we saw, we conjured!"

■

Q: Why did the player attack the tiny slime?

A: She wanted a slimeball to make a brewing potion!

Q: What did the slime say to the player who pushed him off a cliff?

A: "I'll get you next *slime*!"

■

Q: What sound does a witch make when she cries?

A: *Brew-hoo, brew-hoo.*

■

Q: What do players call friendly witches?

A: Failures.

■

Q: How did the player make the witch itch?

A: He took away her *w*.

First player: "I heard that the Plains are one of the biomes."
Second player: "Oh, yes, and do they have the Great Plains in Minecraft?"
First player: "No, the Great Plains are located at the great airport!"

■

First player: "I got lost in the Desert Biome."
Second player: "What were you *dune* out there?"

RIDDLES, PUNS, AND MINECRAFT PHRASES

It's a place where you spawn when you begin the game. Where are you?
The Overworld.

I can jump, am adorable to look at, and you may think I'm tame. Who am I?
The killer rabbit!

If you tell a joke in the Forest Biome and nobody laughs, was it a joke?

It's where you start and spend most of your time. Where are you?
In the Overworld.

I am millions of times larger than Earth and have many different types of biomes. What am I?
The Overworld.

I can't enter the Overworld because there is no return portal. Who am I?
An Ender Dragon.

MINECRAFT LIMERICKS, POEMS, AND HAIKUS

The creation of the killer bunny
Is actually quite funny.
Notch made a habit
Watching the killer rabbit
And was inspired by the havoc.

■

A crack and a flash of light
Turned the sky overwhelmingly bright.
My fear grew deeper,
Watching it charge a creeper.
I retreated, full of fright.

■

Charged creepers explode
And emit a blue aura,
Destroying your world.

■

Mooshrooms or mushrooms?
Yes, it's a bit confusing.
Think *moo*, then think cow!

■

There once was a player named Susan.
Her goal was to clear up the confusion!
Food is a mushroom,
A cow is a mooshroom,
And that's her very bright conclusion!

■

There once was a killer bunny,
Who was scary and not at all funny.
Hopping sixteen blocks, you see,
Run away, you must flee.
He wants blood and not your money!

■

No thorn enchantments.
They are totally useless
On killer rabbits.

■

In the Overworld,
Look in abandoned mineshafts
For sparkling diamonds!

■

There once was a player named Fred.
He tumbled and landed on his head.
In a mineshaft he fell,
Woke up and felt swell,
'Cause he found emeralds and a nice bed!

■

There once was a player named Merle
Who accidently threw an Ender pearl.
The result was endermites.
She fled from their deadly bites.
Oh, what a silly, sorry girl!

■

There once was a player named Dee.
She had the last laugh, you see.
Yes, she was slimed by a slime!
That was perfectly fine!
She used the goo for a potion of tea!

■

In the Overworld,
Grass blocks spawn naturally
And behave like dirt.

■

Endermites attack
Within sixteen blocks, I'm told.
Seventeen are safe!

■

His eyes are blood red
And he moves like a spider:
The killer bunny.

DID YOU KNOW . . . ?

Did you know there are three dimensions: Overworld, Nether, and End?

Did you know Nether portals in the Overworld can be used to teleport to the Nether?

Did you know that most mobs can spawn in the Overworld?

CHAPTER 5

JOCKEYS AND BABY ZOMBIE PIGMEN

JOKES

Q: How did the player get the skeleton to jump off the spider?

A: He jumped into water.

■

Q: What's more disgusting than a baby zombie pigman eating a rabbit?

A: A baby zombie pigman eating a whole cow!

■

Q: What's funnier than a baby zombie pigman?

A: A baby zombie pigman dressed up as Notch!

Q: What did the mommy zombie pigman say to the baby zombie pigman?

A: "You have your father's eyes . . . in your mouth!"

■

Q: Who did the baby zombie pigman call after he lost his head?

A: A headhunter!

■

Q: What do polite baby zombie pigmen say when they first see you?

A: "Pleased to eat you!"

■

First player: "Did you hear about the zombie pigman chicken jockey who kept an open mind?"

Second player: "No, what happened?"

First player: "His brains kept falling out!"

■

Q: What did the zombie pigman chicken jockey say during the wrestling match?

A: "Do you want a piece of me?"

Q. What did one spider jockey say to the other spider jockey?

A: Time flies when you're having flies!

■

Q: Why did the skeleton jump on the spider?

A: He wanted to take it for a spin.

■

Q: What do spider jockeys do when they get angry?

A: They go up the wall!

■

Q: Why was the player so calm when he saw the spider jockey on his keyboard?

A: It was under Ctrl.

■

Q: Why did the minecart accelerate?

A: Because the driver was a spider jockey!

Q: Why was the player acting so cool around the spider jockey?

A: It was daytime!

■

Q: Why do spider jockeys hate winter?

A: Because the cold goes right through them.

■

Q: What did the spider jockey say when he broke his new web?

A: Darn it!

■

Q: Why was the wither skeleton jockey so calm?

A: Because nothing gets under his skin!

Q: Why did the wither skeleton jockey cross the road?

A: To get to the body shop!

■

Q: Who is a wither skeleton jockey's favorite *Star Trek* character?

A: Bones.

■

Q: What did the player who spotted a wither skeleton jockey cross the road do?

A: She jumped out of her skin and joined him!

■

Q: What did the angry wither skeleton jockey call the player?

A: A bonehead!

■

Q: What do you call a crazy chicken jockey?

A: A cuckoo cluck.

Q: What type of cars would chicken jockeys drive?
A: Coupes!

■

Q: How do chicken jockeys slow dance?
A: Chick to chick!

■

Q: Why did the chicken jockey cross the road?
A: Because all the other chicken jockeys were doing it, and he wanted to fit in!

■

Q: Where do chicken jockeys come from?
A: Notch's imagination!

■

Q: What do you call a ghostly chicken jockey?
A: *Poultrygeist*!

■

Q: What did the chicken jockey get an award for?
A: *Deadication*!

Q: Why did the player find a disembodied head inside the piano?

A: A chicken jockey forgot it when he was playing by ear!

■

Q: Why was the player afraid of the skeleton after he killed the spider?

A: He knew the skeleton would continue to attack.

Q: Why was the chicken jockey so good at defeating players?
A: He was quite *deadicated!*

■

Q: What should you do if a chicken jockey comes through your front door?
A: Run through your back door!

TONGUE TWISTERS

Spiders sometimes slither and spawn sideways.

Speedy spiders spun spiderwebs.

Wise spiders weave weaves wonderfully.

Seven silly spiders spin silky socks.

Carla's chicken chose carrots.

Robert rode 'round rumbling roads.

MINECRAFT LIMERICKS, POEMS, AND HAIKUS

A wither skeleton jockey,
His built was rather stocky.
He turned a player named Chuck
Into a very big puck.
He now enjoys playing hockey!

■

There once was a player named Snyder.
His eyes grew big as he spied her.
A skeleton of great height
Gave him a terrible fright!
'Cause he was riding a giant spider!

■

The spider jockey
Is elusive and deadly.
He will shoot and bite.

■

A baby zombie
Or baby zombie pigman
Will ride a chicken!

■

Who rides on its back:
A wither skeleton or
A plain skeleton?

■

Wither skeletons
Are tougher and scarier
Than plain skeletons!

■

Wither skeletons
Walk quite slowly when idle
And sprint, seeing you.

■

A chicken jockey
Despawns and will not lay eggs.
Yet, they can still breed.

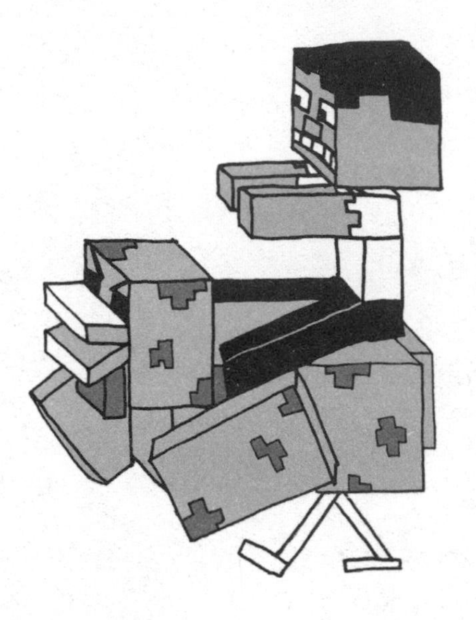

Rare chicken jockeys
Are scary baby zombies
Riding a chicken.

■

Spider jockeys spawn
In tight, narrow enclosures.
Often suffocate!

RIDDLES, PUNS, AND MINECRAFT PHRASES

I have a 0.1 percent chance of spawning. Who am I?
A chicken jockey!

I enjoy running around and I act a lot more like a zombie than a chicken. What am I?
A chicken jockey.

I am the most common jockey in Minecraft. Who am I?
A spider jockey.

I am the least common jockey. Who am I?
An Enderman jockey.

Do spider jockeys wear spider jockstraps?

CHAPTER 6

SWORDS, POTIONS, AND BOWS AND ARROWS

JOKES

Q: What did the creeper say when he nearly got shot by a player's arrow?

A: "Wow; that was an *arrow* escape."

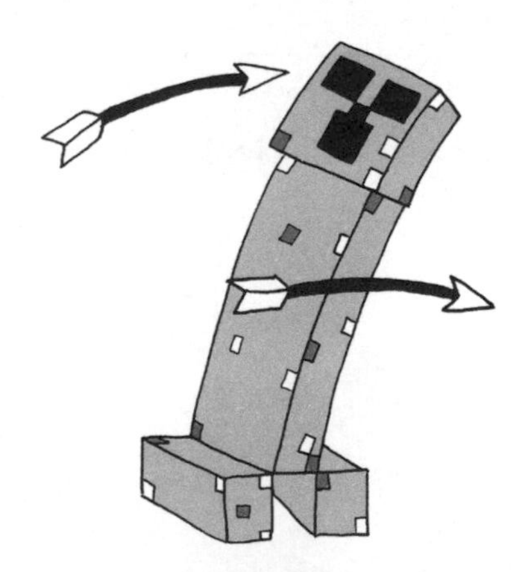

Q: How does Steve tie his shoes?

A: With a long bow!

■

Q: Why was the arrow angry?

A: Because his bow was cross!

■

Q: Why are sticks and string as deadly as sticks and stones?

A: Because with sticks and string you can craft bows!

■

Q: Why was the player shocked that her splash potion of harming didn't kill the skeleton?

A: Because skeletons are immune to splash potion!

■

Q: How did the player keep from getting hurt while battling a blaze?

A: He used a potion of fire resistance!

■

Q: What do you call a creeper in a pool of lava?

A: Destroyed!

Q: What did the creeper say when he destroyed the player who took an invisibility potion?

A: "Move along, nothing to see here."

■

Q: How could the creeper tell that the invisible player was right in front of him?

A: From his farts!

■

Q: How are Minecraft players even more powerful than superheroes?

A: Every day they survive several apocalypses!

■

Q: Instead of taking an invisibility potion, how did the Minecraft player develop the power of becoming invisible?

A: He turned invisible when no one was looking at him!

■

Q: Why is leather armor the best for sneaking?

A: It's made of *hide*!

Q: Why did the witch never get her enchantments right?
A: She kept on forgetting to use spell-check!

■

First player: "Mines are fair and fatal to all players."
Second player: "How so?"
First player: "They are equal opportunity weapons."

■

First player: "I'm not a big fan of archery."
Second player: "Why?"
First player: "It has too many drawbacks."

■

First player: "You know the saying, 'The pen is mightier than the sword?'"
Second player: "Yes, what about it?"
First player: "Well, the person who said it never encountered an angry creeper with a sword!"

First player: "Please pass the salt."

Second player: "What for?"

First player: "So I can *a salt* with a deadly weapon."

■

First player: "I invited my brother to play Minecraft with me."

Second player: "How's it going?"

First player: "Great, he makes a good moving target!"

■

First player: "I have an archery joke."

Second player: "I'd love to hear it."

First player: "I'm not sure if it's quite on target. I could make one, but I don't really see the point."

■

Q: Why was everyone able to see the player who took the invisibility potion?

A: Because she forgot to take off her armor!

■

First player: "I went online and asked a store carrying Minecraft merchandise if they had any free merchandise."
Second player: "Did you get any?"
First player: "No, they blocked me!"

■

Q: Why couldn't the player hit the ghast?
A: Because his arrows were all *a quiver*.

First player: "I was in a play at school and I forgot my line."
Second player: "What did you do?"
First player: "I shouted 'Minecraft' because I wanted to say something constructive!"

MINECRAFT LIMERICKS, POEMS, AND HAIKUS

With hopes of creating a potion,
A player came up with a notion.
She took two instead of one.
Good news, no harm was done,
'Cause many potions resets one's motions!

■

Arrows on the ground
Will move, even if untouched,
Right toward the player!

■

Arrows catch fire
When shot through hot, hot lava,
but not through fire!

■

Arrows won't collide
If shot at Nether portals.
They often skip through.

■

Iron sword's texture
Came before the other swords.
Then more swords followed.

■

When blocking players,
Vertical moves speed remains,
Even if you fly.

■

Enchanted silk touch
Makes your sword collect cobwebs.
When using commands.

■

There once was a player named Mae.
Her arrows often did stray.
While shooting at creepers,
And missing their peepers,
Mae became the creepers' prey!

■

A player came up with a notion.
He created an enchanted potion.
His aim was to tame
Ender Dragons and seek fame.
Instead, he caused a commotion.

■

Careful where you aim.
Arrows will fly to the right.
Bows are off-center.

■

There once was a player named Moe.
He loved shooting arrows with his bow.
He aimed at a ghast.
The arrows flew past.
One landed on his giant big toe!

■

An excellent maker of potions
Caused a bit of commotion
When he mixed up a quart
Of melon and Nether wart.
Bad tasting, he threw it in the ocean!

■

A player who lost all feeling,
Mixed up a potion of healing.
Ingredients she scanned.
Everything was at hand.
At last she's strong and appealing.

■

There once was a player named Nell.
At night she often stumbled and fell.
She made a decision
To fix her poor night vision.
A potion made her feel swell!

■

There once was a player named Trevor.
He was incredibly clever.
He caused a commotion
With a deadly potion.
Now hostile mobs fear him forever.

■

The potion made the zombie quake.
He stumbled and fell in a lake.
The player could bet
He wasn't dead yet,
Because he saw the zombie shake.

■

Mixing splash potions of harming
Can be incredibly alarming.
On some, it has no effect,
So you better elect
To find other ways of disarming!

■

Imagine Justin's giddy glee,
Turning fermented spider eye to tea!
Mixed with golden carrot
And adding Nether wart,
He's invisible and no one can see!

■

There once was a player named Jack.
One thing that he never did lack,
For he had a gift
and was incredibly swift.
With sugar and Nether wart, he made tracks!

■

Don't apply logic
When mixing new splash potions—
That's what Jeb will say!

■

Hah! Trying to kill
Fierce Endermen and blazes—
Splash potions won't work.

RIDDLES, PUNS, AND MINECRAFT PHRASES

I can be made of wood, stone, gold, iron, and diamonds. What am I?
Swords.

I can be crafted with leather, gold, fire, iron, and diamonds. What am I?
Armor.

I bounce off minecarts and some mobs. What am I?
An arrow!

I am more powerful at breaking blocks than your fists. What am I?
A sword!

You can't see me when I'm working. What am I?
A pen with an invisibility potion!

When I blow up and an arrow passes by, I can change the arrow's direction. What am I?
TNT!

I help players hold their breath longer when they are underwater. What am I?
Water-breathing potion, which contains Nether wart and a raw pufferfish.

DID YOU HEAR . . . ?

Did you hear about the player who took the invisibility potion?
He was nothing to look at!

Did you hear about the player who tried to stick an arrow into the ground?
He couldn't see the point.

CHAPTER 7

SURVIVAL

JOKES

Q: Why is it bad to feed round bales of hay to Minecraft cows?

A: Because they won't get a square meal!

■

Q: What did the Minecraft player say after breaking rocks?

A: "I smashed it into total *obsidian*!"

■

Q: What did the polite Minecraft sheep named Elvis say after he was fed?

A: "Thank ewe very much!"

■

Q: Why did the Minecraft player label the rabbit?

A: He wanted a piece of toast.

Q: What do you get when you pour hot water down a rabbit hole?

A: Hot-cross bunnies.

■

Q: Why did the player run around the house?

A: She was running away from a creeper.

Q: What do you call a rude Minecraft cow?

A: Beef jerky.

■

Q: What's the best thing to put into pumpkin pie?

A: Your teeth!

Q: When is a pumpkin not a pumpkin?

A: When you drop it. Then, it's squash!

■

Q: Do you know what a good Minecraft balanced diet is?

A: A cookie in each hand!

■

Q: Why couldn't the player reach the roof?

A: He tried to climb up his house without a ladder!

■

Q: Why couldn't the player run around?

A: Because in Minecraft, nothing is round!

■

Q: How did the player who ate raw chicken get rid of food poisoning?

A: He drank milk!

■

Q: Why did the player break the leaves of the oak tree?

A: Because he was hungry and wanted to eat apples!

Q: What do you get when you cross a cat with a squid?

A: *Cat-amari*!

■

Q: How does an apple a day keep the ghast away?

A: When you take perfect aim!

■

Q: How do you make an apple puff?

A: Chase it around your garden!

■

Q: How do you hide an Ender Dragon?

A: Paint his toenails red and put him in an apple orchard!

■

Q: What kind of keys do players like to carry?

A: Cookies!

■

Q: What is blue and purple and crawls through a field?

A: Steve looking for his lost cookies!

Q: Why did Steve only bake one cookie?

A: Because he ate the rest of the dough!

■

Q: How did the Minecraft player make the stew richer?

A: He added fourteen carrots!

■

Q: What did the players get when they played tug-of-war with a pig?

A: Pulled pork!

■

Q: What did one player say when he swiped the cake from his opponent?

A: "That was a piece of cake!"

■

Q: How do Minecraft witches style their hair?

A: With scare spray!

■

Q: How do you make your meals richer?

A: Add karats!

Q: What's invisible and smells like carrots?

A: Bunny farts!

■

Q: How did the Minecraft player communicate with fish?

A: He dropped a line.

■

Q: How does a creeper say hello?

A: "Kaboom!"

■

Q: Why did the witch stand up in front of the other witches?

A: Because she had to give a *screech*.

■

Q: If there was a national anthem for Minecraft, what would it be?

A: "I Will Survive!"

Q: How is a Minecraft player like a person meditating?

A: When they eat, both say, "Om!"

■

Q: Why are carrots thin and pointy?

A: Because if they were round, they wouldn't be in Minecraft.

■

Q: What do you get when you cross a fishing rod with a player's dirty sock?

A: A hook, line, and stinker!

■

Q: Why did the zombie pigman go to the dentist?

A: To improve his bite.

■

Q: How did the player get hold of a potato?

A: He killed a zombie!

■

Q: What do you call a potato that you steal from a zombie?

A: A hot potato!

Q: What did the player call a baby potato?

A: Small fry!

■

Q: Which way did the player carrying a bunch of potatoes travel?

A: He took the fork in the road!

■

Q: What does Taylor Swift sing when she plays Minecraft and eats potatoes?

A: "Taters gonna tate!"

■

Q: What's the difference between potatoes and zombies?

A: You can't mash zombies!

■

Q: What do you get when you cross a potato with a hostile mob?

A: Mashed potatoes!

■

Q: How does Guy Fieri make the best pickles?

A: He uses Herobrine!

Q: Who was the guest of honor at the Brine family reunion?
A: Herobrine!

■

Q: What did one player say to the other who wasn't doing a good job flying?
A: "That's not flying; that's falling!"

■

First player: "Did you know that takeoffs are optional?"
Second player: "Yes, and landing is mandatory!"

■

First player: "Did you know flying isn't dangerous?"
Second player: "Of course! *Crashing* is dangerous!"

■

Q: Who does Superman look up to?
A: Herobrine!

First player: "Most people would think that flying is the greatest thrill."
Second player: "It's not?"
First player: "Nope. It's landing!"

■

First player: "If you build it, they will come!"
Second player: "Yes, but that means creepers, ghasts, and other hostile mobs, too!"

■

First player: "My friends and I were so nervous constructing our first Minecraft tower."
Second player: "I know. The buildup was intense!"

■

First player: "Vegetables are a must on my diet!"
Second player: "Mine, too. I suggest we start with pumpkin pie!"

■

First player: "Do you like baked apples?"
Second player: "Yes, I do. Why?"
First player: "That's good, because your orchard's on fire."

First player: "Did you hear about the apple that the creeper threw that stopped in midair?"
Second player: "No, what happened?"
First player: "It ran out of juice!"

■

First player: "If it took six pigs two hours to eat carrots in the field, how many hours would it take three pigs?"
Second player: "None, because the six pigs would have eaten all of them!"

■

First player: "What is the left side of an apple?"
Second player: "The side that you don't eat!"

■

First player: "How do you make an apple turnover?"
Second player: "You push it down a hill."

■

First player: "I upgraded my armor."
Second player: "How'd you do that?"
First player: "They were having a sale for one *knight* only!"

Knock, knock

Who's there?

You're a diamond?

You're a diamond who?

You're a *diamond* me crazy!

Knock, knock.

Who's there?

Carrot.

Carrot, who?

Do you *carrot* all about me?

MINECRAFT LIMERICKS, POEMS, AND HAIKUS

There once was a player named Faye.
Wandering off the path, she did stray.
She opened a portal
And met an immortal.
Now, Faye is not doing okay!

■

There once was a builder named Marie,
She went on a building spree.
She encountered some creepers,
Who acted like grim reapers,
So Marie decided to flee.

■

It might sound creepy, so you say,
That I spend time killing zombies each day.
It's not a profession.
It's more like an obsession.
That's why I play all night and all day!

■

There once was a player named Alice.
Sometimes she was quite callous.
Her stomach was tough.
The puffer she ate was rough.
Now poor Alice was filled with malice!

■

The ghast, he started to cry
When the player asked him, "Why?"
He answered, "The food
Is tasteless and crude."
He would have preferred pumpkin pie!

■

A village butcher
Will trade seven cooked pork chops
For an emerald.

■

Clownfish taste funny.
Players will eat them uncooked.
It is like sushi.

■

Throw back the puffer.
Eating it will poison you
And make you hungry.

■

You make mushroom stew
By milking mooshrooms with bowls.
Then you eat, om nom!

■

Tame, breed, grow, and heal
Horses with golden carrots.
Bunnies like them, too!

■

It's not at all true
That golden carrot potions
Can cure night vision.

RIDDLES, PUNS, AND MINECRAFT PHRASES

I am made of diamonds, obsidian, and a book. What am I?
An enchantment table.

I spawn underground. What am I?
A mineshaft.

The more you take from it, the larger it gets. What am I?
A ditch.

I move silently without wings, and I hang on strong strings. What am I?
A spider.

First you see me in the grass dressed in yellow. When I'm a dainty white, I fly away. What am I?
A dandelion.

I am quite nutritious if you cook me in a furnace. What am I?
A cod.

I'm very tempting to eat, and my skin is red. What am I?
An apple.

You will become hungry after eating me. What am I?
A pufferfish.

I must die so you can live. What am I?
An animal that drops food.

Why do we bake cookies and cook bacon?

The player who stole my cookie really took the biscuit!

What food restores some of your hunger and at the same time depletes your hunger meter at a faster rate?
Rotting flesh!

CHAPTER 8

CREATIVE

JOKES

Q: What is Steve and Alex's favorite song?

A: "We Built This City."

■

Q: Why did the player bring gold and silver into his boat?

A: He needed ores!

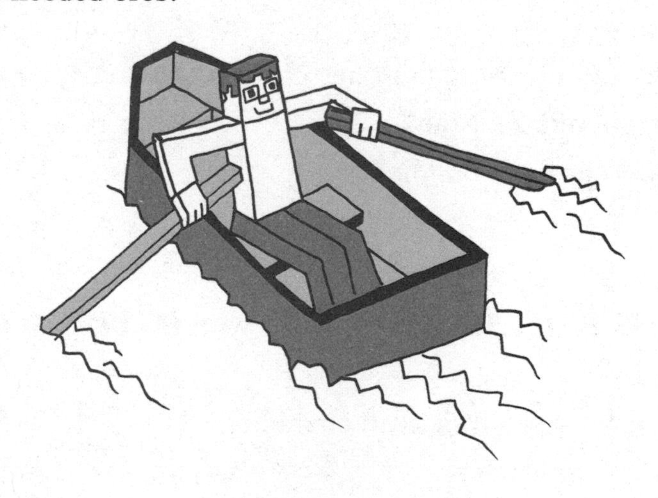

Q: Why did Steve's white shirt turn blue?
A: Because he washed it with lapis in the pockets!

■

Q: What's the difference between a good landing and a great landing?
A: In Minecraft a good landing is where you can walk away, and a great landing is when you have no injuries!

■

Q: How do you measure a Minecraft player's shoe size?
A: In square feet.

■

Q: Why did the mom help her child create a Minecraft version of Iron Man?
A: It was character building.

■

Q: What did the Minecraft player with the blocked nose say?
A: "I wish I was a Minecraft character!"

Q: How do Minecraft players stay calm?

A: They take a walk around the block!

■

Q: What happened to the player who was hit by a piano?

A: He became *A-flat minor*!

Q: What's the tallest building in Minecraft?

A: The library, because it has the most stories!

■

Q: Why was the player barking up the wrong tree?

A: Because he was *stumped* that it *wooden* give him wood!

First player: "My login password is CreeperGhastSteveandAlex."
Second player: "Why is it so long?"
First player: "It has to have at least four characters."

■

Knock, knock,
Who's there?
Theodore.
Theodore who?
Theodore was open, so I'm coming in!

■

Q: What did the player say while rolling down a bumpy road?
A: "I can feel my *cart* pounding!"

MINECRAFT LIMERICKS, POEMS, AND HAIKUS

There once was a player named Roy.
He loved to build and destroy
With much creativity
And productivity,
Which, in creative, he would employ!

■

A player was exploring a cave.
He had a very close shave.
He stepped on a cave spider,
Who was a great fighter.
Fortunately, he was faster than brave!

■

There once was a player named Lou.
His dream was to build a big zoo.
He filled it with pigs and sheep,
And even creepers that creep—
Playing Minecraft, he knew just what to do!

■

A player named Katie was quite skilled.
She knew what she wanted to build:
A castle so high
That would reach the sky.
Now her dream was completely fulfilled.

■

There one was player named Joan.
She dreamed of building a home.
A great imagination,
She crafted a sensation
That she created all on her own!

■

Creative allows
All players to destroy blocks.
You can also fly.

■

Falling through a hole
Happens in bedrock layer
In Creative mode.

■

Tap the space bar twice
So you fly up near the top.
Shift makes you go down.

■

In Creative mode,
Just be careful not to fall
Into the dark void.

■

Flying above clouds,
You can see the sun and moon.
Both are visible.

■

Flying high enough,
You can spot the sun and moon
When looking downward!

RIDDLES, PUNS, AND MINECRAFT PHRASES

Always remember to keep the number of landings you make equal to the number of takeoffs you've made!

When flying, always remember that good judgment comes from experience. Unfortunately, experience comes from bad judgment!

I sleep all day and fly by night. I have no feathers. What am I?
A bat.

There's no hunger or ill health. Where am I?
In Creative mode!

I am optional and mandatory. What am I?
Takeoffs and landings!

I can be used to free up large outdoor areas and get rid of grass. What am I?
A bucket of water!

I can slow you down and make a good trap for hostile mobs. What am I?
Soul sand.

I am a good tool for building underwater and preventing leaks. What am I?
A ladder!

You can carry all of your food, but you can't eat it here. Where are you?
Creative mode!

You are out of blocks and can still build with me. What am I?
The side of a torch!

I will help you breath underwater. What am I?
A torch.

DID YOU KNOW . . . ?

Did you know you can have unlimited items in Creative mode?

Did you know you can fly in Creative mode?

Did you know that, in Creative mode, you can't die unless you fall into the void?

Did you know that, in the Pocket Edition, if you die in Creative mode, you get to keep your entire inventory?

Did you know that torches create temporary air pockets underwater?

Did you know that torches can break stacks of sand and gravel?

Did you know that you can use a torch to hold up sand and gravel?

Did you know that ladders and signs can stop water and lava from flowing?

Did you know that blazes hate snowballs?

Did you know that soul sand can make you sink?

Did you know that just two buckets of water will give you an infinite supply of water?

CHAPTER 9

PEACEFUL TO THE END

JOKES

Q: Why couldn't the hostile mob spawn?

A: Because he was in Peaceful mode.

■

Q: What do you call a cow that works on a Minecraft player's yard?

A: A lawn *moo-er*.

■

Q: Why was the Old West gunfighter such a fan of Minecraft?

A: He liked to put a notch in his six shooter!

Q: What did one witch say to the other?

A: "Your potion *blew* me away!"

■

Q: What did the player say to the Ender Dragon?

A: "You want a *peace* of me?"

■

Q: What did the competitive Minecraft coach say to his youngest player?

A: "There's no crying in Minecraft."

Q: What did President Obama say the first time he played Minecraft?

A: Who knows? The press never covers the really important stuff.

■

Q: What's a Minecraft player's favorite car?

A: The Nissan Cube!

■

Q: What can make a Minecraft player cry?

A: Nothing. We're really tough!

■

Q: What did the zombie see when he pulled down the Enderman's trousers?

A: *Ender*pants!

Q: What can make a Minecraft player cry?

A: Everything. We're really sensitive!

■

Q: What did the player call the deaf Ender Dragon?

A: Anything he wanted, because the Ender Dragon couldn't hear him!

■

Q: What do you get when an Ender Dragon sneezes?

A: Out of the way!

■

Q: Where do you go when an Ender Dragon farts?

A: Far, far away!

■

Q: Why did the Ender Dragon cross the road?

A: Because chickens weren't invented yet!

■

Q: What powers do Minecraft players have?

A: Incredible ones, because they keep on surviving the End!

Q: Why can't Minecraft players spell Armageddon?

A: Because it's not the End!

■

Q: What song will players sing at the End?

A: "It's the End of the World."

■

First player: "I want to start in Hardcore mode."

Second player: "All I am saying is give *peace* a chance!"

First player: "What song lyrics do Minecraft players like to sing?"
Second player: "And now the End is here, and I have faced my final battle, and did it Notch's way!"

■

First player: "I heard the End has its own soundtrack."
Second player: "What does it sound like?"
First player: "You can only hear it in the End."

MINECRAFT LIMERICKS, POEMS, AND HAIKUS

John started off in Peaceful mode.
He built a very grand abode.
No fears from hostile creatures—
This mode it didn't feature,
Except one Ender Dragon on this road.

■

A player went up to the next level.
He thought he encountered the devil.
Please, don't be so daft!
There's no devil in Minecraft.
Just a ghast, which is on the same level!

■

There once was a player named Shirl.
She found an Ender pearl.
She dreamed of transporting
And thought it was very sporting.
She threw it and gave it a whirl!

■

There once was a player named Al.
He was everyone's favorite pal.
He tamed an Ender Dragon,
Who now drives his wagon,
And the dragon lives in Al's corral!

■

Want to teleport?
You should throw an Ender pearl
And you will arrive!

■

Hostile mobs can spawn
And create lots of damage.
This is quite normal.

■

When difficulty
Is set to peaceful level,
Hostile mobs won't spawn.

■

Ender pearls that fall
Into the void won't trigger
You to teleport.

■

A stark empty plane;
A floating planet island.
It is called the End.

■

Lava flows faster,
It's just like in the Nether,
Only in the End.

■

An endless, dark sky,
With a huge mass of end stone,
Looks like a deep void.

■

You'll find small islands
And obsidian pillars
Scattered in the End!

■

Exploding beds start
Fires and portals won't work
When you reach the End.

RIDDLES AND PUNS

My poison is useless in easy mode. Who am I?
A cave spider.

I flow faster in the End and in the Nether. What am I?
Lava.

At night they appear without being fetched. By day they are gone without being stolen. What are they?
Stars.

When I break, I sound just like shattered glass. What am I?
An End portal frame.

When I am slain, I drop one Ender pearl. Who am I?
An Enderman.

I have a 5 percent chance of spawning endermites. What am I?
An Ender pearl.

Villagers no longer use me and I craft the eyes. What am I?
Ender pearls.

The day to night cycle doesn't exist. Where are you?
At the End!

All of the crystals are destroyed and I am powerless. Who am I?
The Ender Dragon.

How can you create an exit portal from the End?
Destroy the Ender Dragon.

Clocks and compasses spin randomly and if you try to sleep in a bed it will explode. Where are you?
The End!

DID YOU KNOW . . . ?

Did you know that if you ride a minecart into an active End portal, it won't take you to the End?

Did you know that if you exit that cart, you will be sent to the End?

Did you know that if you destroy the frame, the portal will still work?

Did you know that if you spawn an Ender Dragon outside of the End, the dragon will drop an exit portal, taking you to the End?

Did you know that if you want to find the End, the first thing you need to do is first find and then complete an End portal?

CHAPTER 10

RESPAWNING

JOKES

Q: Why did the Minecraft player continue to play football with a broken leg?

A: He was waiting to respawn.

■

Q: Why didn't the Minecraft player immediately text back her friend?

A: She was waiting to respawn!

■

Q: What did the player say when he saw the same creeper who recently destroyed him?

A: "You are a blast from my past!"

Q: Why will the world never end?

A: Because Minecraft players keep on respawning.

■

Q: What did the Minecraft player wish for?

A: To respawn as Steve!

■

Q: What type of circle do Minecraft players love?

A: The circle of life!

■

Q: What happened to the player who became totally absorbed with Minecraft?

A: He entered *nerdvana*!

■

Q: What did the Minecraft player say to the player who died for the first time?

A: "I didn't believe in respawning at first, either!"

■

Q: What's a Minecraft player's favorite song?

A: "Karma Chameleon," because players keep on coming and going.

Q: What are the two things Minecraft players can count on?

A: Destruction and respawning!

■

Q: What happens right before witches respawn?

A: They go away for a spell!

■

Q: What did the Minecraft player say right before he was destroyed?

A: "I'll be right back!"

■

Q: What did the respawned player say?

A: "Did and done that before!"

■

Q: What is a respawned player's favorite song lyrics?

A: "A whole new world."

■

Q: What did one player say to the other?

A: "I've heard respawning is making a comeback!"

Q: What is the most popular phrase in Minecraft?
A: "You died!"

■

Q: What's the difference between a cat and a Minecraft player?
A: A cat only has nine lives!

■

Q: What did the ghast say to the player who died and respawned?
A: "Déjà Boo!"

■

Q: Why did the player wish he could take his math test in Minecraft?
A: Because if he failed, he could have a do-over!

■

Q: How do you keep a monster from respawning?
A: Stick a name tag on him.

■

Q: What did the creeper say to the respawned player?
A: "I think we've met before!"

Q: What movie don't Minecraft players get?

A: The James Bond movie, *You Only Live Twice*.

■

Q: How is Minecraft like déjà vu?

A: Every time you play the game, you feel like you've been here before.

■

Q: What song lyrics do Minecraft players like to sing?

A: "We have all been here before!"

■

Q: What is a Minecraft player's worst nightmare?

A: Losing the ability to respawn!

■

First player: "Why did the player feel immortal?"
Second player: "I don't know, why?"
First player: "Because Minecraft gamers keep on respawning!"

■

First player: "If a player was born in Sweden, raised in America, and died in Mexico, what does that make him?"
Second player: "Deceased."

■

First player: "What's do you eat before you die?"
Second player: "You bite the dust!"

■

First player: "I had a near death experience."
Second player: "What happened?"
First player: "I escaped from a zombie attack, and then saw Notch!"

■

First player: "Have you heard the jokes about immortality?"
Second player: "No, I haven't."
First player: "That's too bad. They never get old!"

■

First player: "I found something round in Minecraft!"
Second player: "You did? What?"
First player: "A circle of life!"

■

First player: "There's a first time for everything . . ."
Second player: "Except when you respawn!"

■

First player: "Studies show that for every fifteen minutes you laugh, you gain an extra day of life."
Second player: "That's nothing. In Minecraft, we respawn every time we are destroyed!"

■

First player: "Time is a great healer."
Second player: "That's true, but in Minecraft, you keep on respawning!"

MINECRAFT LIMERICKS, POEMS, AND HAIKUS

There once was a player named Lou.
This land seems familiar, it's true!
He felt pretty sure
He had been here before.
This is what's called déjà vu!

■

The player with an old computer,
Couldn't plug in her new router;
It wouldn't unlock
And gave her a shock.
She died, and I had to reboot her!

■

The Minecraft player had died.
In her gaming skills, she took deep pride.
Happy and reborn,
This she soon had sworn:
"I'll learn from my mistakes!" she cried.

■

There once was player named Belle.
While battling ghasts, she fell.
But while falling she gave a yawn.
She knew she would respawn.
And in her new skin, she felt swell.

■

She lost a battle
And fell straight down with a splat!
Don't fret; she respawned.

■

When life is quite bad,
All we really have to do
Is stop and reboot!

RIDDLES, PUNS, AND MINECRAFT PHRASES

Why do Minecraft players like the number thirty-two?

Because hostile mobs cease to exist if you are within thirty-two blocks of them for more than thirty seconds!

Best excuse ever: "I didn't call you back because I was waiting to respawn!"

The player was so sure he would respawn that he wrote a will leaving everything to himself!

You know you've been playing Minecraft too long when your hands start to bleed and you can't figure out why you haven't respawned.

There's a first time for everything, except as a Minecraft player respawning!

After being destroyed again, the Minecraft player said, BRB (Be Right Back) instead of RIP.

Can Minecraft players get déjà vu?

Respawning isn't like amnesia. You remember and keep on getting better!

If at first you don't succeed, respawn, respawn again!

Respawning is so fun that you keep on doing it over and over again!

Keep calm and respawn!

Great players don't really die. They keep on respawning!

By respawning, we learn from our mistakes!

CHAPTER 11

YOU MIGHT BE A MINECRAFT ADDICT IF . . .

You might be a Minecraft addict if your friends and family call you a blockhead and you don't mind.

You might be a Minecraft addict if you try to make things out of your cubed carrots.

You might be a Minecraft addict if you punch trees to gather wood for your fireplace.

You might be a Minecraft addict if you scour gravel driveways in search of flint.

You might be a Minecraft addict if you put sand in the oven, hoping it will turn into glass.

You might be a Minecraft addict if you argue with your science teacher, who says trees really do have roots and branches.

You might be a Minecraft addict if you sleep in Minecraft when you are tired in real life.

You might be a Minecraft addict if you go outside in the snow dressed in a T-shirt and pants.

You might be a Minecraft addict if you get upset that the tree you planted in your backyard takes months to grow.

You might be a Minecraft addict if you arrange your school supplies in groups of sixty-four.

You might be a Minecraft addict if you've built tunnels under your home looking for coal and iron.

You might be a Minecraft addict if you get coal for your birthday and think it's a great gift.

You might be addicted to Minecraft if you know more about the game than about your school work.

You might be a Minecraft addict if you've taken up cactus gardening and you don't live in a dry biome.

You might be a Minecraft addict if you start digging for glowstone to save energy.

You might be a Minecraft addict if you write Minecraft fanfiction for your English essay.

You might be a Minecraft addict if you've read and critiqued other Minecraft players' fanfiction.

You might be a Minecraft addict if your wardrobe consists of simple T-shirts and purple pants.

You might be a Minecraft addict if you can't understand why your farm doesn't tend to itself.

You might be a Minecraft addict if all four walls in your room have at least one picture of Steve and Alex.

You might be a Minecraft addict if you add a trap door in your room to hide from invading creepers.

You might be a Minecraft addict if you don't own anything that is round.

You might be a Minecraft addict if you petition your school to add Swedish as a language requirement.

You might be a Minecraft addict if you study Swedish with the goal of getting updates faster.

You might be a Minecraft addict if you only listen to Minecraft music on your iPod.

You might be a Minecraft addict if you watch YouTube Minecraft videos hourly.

You might be a Minecraft addict if you tell your friends and everyone you meet that they can build anything.

You might be a Minecraft addict if all your clocks just show when dusk and dawn happen.

You might be a Minecraft addict if your greatest ambition is to be Steve.

You might be a Minecraft addict if you start building a watch that just says "dusk" and "dawn."

You might be a Minecraft addict if you argue with a farmer that wool comes from punching sheep.

You might be a Minecraft addict is you sit too close to the screen and your eyes are now square.

You might be a Minecraft addict if you get nostalgic about Indev.

You might be a Minecraft addict if you get confused when you see a ball roll.

You might be a Minecraft addict if you spend hours searching for Herobrine.

You might be a Minecraft addict if you spend every waking moment thinking about Minecraft.

You might be a Minecraft addict if you dream in pixels.

You might be a Minecraft addict if you mistake your dog for a sheep.

You might be a Minecraft addict if you vacation at the beach and spend all of your time punching the sand.

You might be a Minecraft addict if you picture everything in blocks and pixels.

You might be a Minecraft addict if you decorate your room by stacking everything into blocks.

You might be a Minecraft addict if you refuse to make eye contact with tall people dressed in black.

You might be a Minecraft addict if your mom tells you to clean your room and instead you clean up the house you just created.

You might be a Minecraft addict if you forget to give your mom a present for her birthday and instead get her a Minecraft account XD.

You might be a Minecraft addict if you wake up on a real airplane, look out the window, and are convinced you are looking at a world hole.

You might be a Minecraft addict if you get confused when your friends talk about other things to do on a computer.

You might be a Minecraft addict if you are home alone and turn on all of the lights because you are convinced that creepers spawn in real life!

You might be a Minecraft addict if you think the world is square.

You might be a Minecraft addict if you have a shrine to Notch in your room.

You might be a Minecraft addict if you go to a farm and are confused why the sheep, pigs, and horses aren't square.

You might be a Minecraft addict if you hear the words: block, mine, coal, bedrock, craft, biome, village, or survival, and immediately think of Minecraft.

You might be a Minecraft addict if you meet a guy named Steve and ask him if he's related to the *real* Steve.

You might be a Minecraft addict if you believe you are a world traveler because of the places you've built.

You might be a Minecraft addict if you hear a *boom* outside your window and think it's a creeper.

You might be a Minecraft addict if you sleep with the lights on because you are afraid of creepers.

You might be a Minecraft addict if you wake up in the middle of the night and want to light a torch.

You might be a Minecraft addict if you hear a *sssssss* coming from the TV and you run to get your bow and arrow.

You might be a Minecraft addict if you get a high score at the Minecraft Addiction test site.

You might be a Minecraft addict if you place torches everywhere around your house so nothing spawns in it.

You might be a Minecraft addict if you place a plank of wood at your front door, thinking it will open as soon as you step on it.

You might be a Minecraft addict if you buy only fifteen feet of wire because you think it will lose power after fifteen feet.

You might be a Minecraft addict if you look at a brick building and think, *Man, that's a lot of clay!*

You might be a Minecraft addict if you go to a farm and try to saddle a pig so you can ride it.

You might be a Minecraft addict if you try to make your own water supply by putting one bucket of water at each end of a hole you dug.

You might be a Minecraft addict if you broke your glasses and thought, *Oh no, what texture pack is this?*

You might be a Minecraft addict if you throw a snowball at a sheep and expect wool or a clock to drop.

You might be a Minecraft addict if your best friend is wearing a great outfit and you ask her where she bought that nice skin.

You might be a Minecraft addict if you admire your friend's skin and ask her where she crafted it.

You might be a Minecraft addict if you look at pictures of faraway places and think, *I can build a nice base there!*

You might be a Minecraft addict if you look at buildings and think how you can craft them.

You might be a Minecraft addict if you dress up in iron pants and don't understand why they are so uncomfortable.

You might be a Minecraft addict if you ask your parents to get you a slime for a pet.

You might be a Minecraft addict if you check the distance to the floor so you don't fall.

You might be a Minecraft addict if you see the sun start to set and you gather sticks to look for coal.

Your might be a Minecraft addict if you form your mashed potatoes into cubes.

You might be a Minecraft addict if you think Pong is a gateway game.

You might be a Minecraft addict if you only play for six hours straight because you are cutting back.

You might be a Minecraft addict if you realize that you've built more buildings than all of the buildings in your state.

You might be a Minecraft addict if you create block-themed holiday decorations.

You might be a Minecraft addict if you're drowning and think you'll respawn.

You might be a Minecraft addict if you hear a noise in the middle of the night and think, *It's okay, I have Peaceful mode on!*

You might be a Minecraft addict if you wonder, *Does this diamond armor make me look too square?*

You might be a Minecraft addict if instead of turning the handle to open the door, you smash it with a pickaxe.

You might be a Minecraft addict if you cut out the middle of a tree and are surprised when it falls.

You might be a Minecraft addict if you get confused by round shapes.

You might be a Minecraft addict if you spill something and put a sign next to it to stop it from spreading.

You might be a Minecraft addict if you throw eggs on the ground and expect to see a chicken.

You might be a Minecraft addict if the tea kettle whistles and you think, *Creeper!*

You might be a Minecraft addict if you drive a boat to the bottom of a waterfall and expect it to be rocketed to the top.

You might be a Minecraft addict if you don't understand why you can't carry all of the groceries in one trip.

You might be a Minecraft addict if you are afraid of pigs because you think one day they will transform into zombie pigmen.

You might be a Minecraft addict if you visit a farm and are surprised that there are no pink or yellow sheep.

You might be a Minecraft addict if you try on new clothes and think, *This* skin *looks great on me!*

You might be a Minecraft addict if you see mossy stone and think it's a dungeon.

You might be a Minecraft addict if you smack snow with a shovel and expect snowballs to pop up.

You might be a Minecraft addict if you hear someone go "Urg" and you ask your friend if he's packing a sword so you can kill a zombie.

You might be a Minecraft addict if you see a sign stating WE BUY GOLD and think, *No way, I'm saving my gold for power rails.*

You might be a Minecraft addict if you see a circle and think, *That's not right.*

You might be a Minecraft addict if you can't think outside the blocks.

You might be a Minecraft addict if you seriously think about becoming an actual miner when you grow up.

You might be a Minecraft addict if you do a double take because you thought you saw a creeper following you, but it turned out to be your little sister.

You might be a Minecraft addict if you hear someone groan and you shout, "Zombie!"

You might be a Minecraft addict if you hear a dog bark and think if you follow the sound, you'll find a pack of wolves.

You might be a Minecraft addict if you ask your mom to replace the light in your room with a torch.

You might be a Minecraft addict if you run away when your cat hisses because you think you heard a creeper.

You might be a Minecraft addict if you spot a water fountain and wish you had a bucket on you.

You might be a Minecraft addict if you sign up for art class just so you could spend your time sketching stuff to build later.

You might be a Minecraft addict if you're young and look forward to turning sixty-four.

You might be a Minecraft addict if someone asks you how big your house is and you answer, "Four chunks!"

You might be a Minecraft addict if you don't understand why your dog doesn't sit when you right click.

You might be a Minecraft addict if you see a spider and are puzzled that it's not as big as you.

You might be a Minecraft addict if you are terrified of thunderstorms because you believe hostile mobs will spawn.

You might be a Minecraft addict if you knew that the game was originally called *Cave Game*.

You might be a Minecraft addict if you knew the creeper started as a coding error.

You might be a Minecraft addict if you put cocoa beans on the kitchen counter, pour milk on them, and expect to make chocolate milk.

You might be a Minecraft addict if you tried to convince your family to move to Stockholm so you could attend the school where Minecraft was made a compulsory part of the curriculum.

You might be a Minecraft addict if you can't read normal clocks.

You might be a Minecraft addict if you look at your pet and think, *Notch has made a new mob!*

You might be a Minecraft addict if your favorite pastime is going to the junkyard to watch them crush cars into cubes.

CHAPTER 12

MINECRAFT SAYINGS WE'D LIKE TO SEE

- Never dig down!
- Ssss! Boom!
- Live life to the fullest. Take it up a Notch!
- Just one more block!
- Another creeper bites the dust!

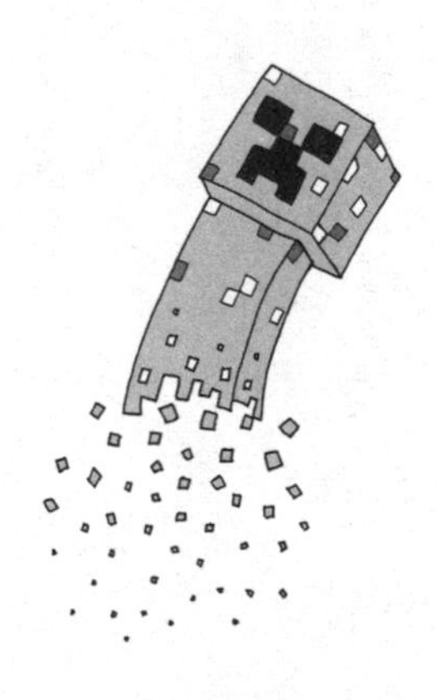

- If you build it, hostile mobs will come!
- Live in your world. Play in mines!
- If you can mine it, you can craft it!
- WWND?
- To be ore not to be?
- Follow me to Nether Nether land.
- We vacation in the Netherlands.
- Ender the Dragon!
- Herobrine the Legend!
- Never hug a creeper!
- I lava you!
- I'd rather be mining!
- A golden apple a day keeps the doctor away!
- Take it up a Notch!
- Minecraft: it's LEGO with zombies!
- Minecraft: what a ghast!
- Minecraft: can you dig it?
- Minecraft: Sandbox 2.0!

- I did Minecraft!
- Give a wolf a bone!
- I'm in a feud with the mob!
- Veni, Vidi, Vici, Minecraft!
- Love is never having to explain Minecraft!
- It's simply Minecraft over matter!
- Minecraft is like a box of chocolates: you never know what's going to get you!
- There's always time for Minecraft!
- Minecraft: think inside and outside the blocks!
- Minecraft: no limit to your imagination!
- I came, I saw, I mined!
- Victory is Mine . . . craft!
- Minecraft: where inspiration never sleeps and Nether do you!
- Success: it's a Mine . . . craft game!
- Herobrine: now you see him, now you don't!
- Minecraft: there is no substitute!
- Minecraft: just play it!

- I ain't afraid of no ghasts!
- Minecraft: where everything is possible!
- Keep on playing those Minecraft games forever!
- Minecraft: think blocks!
- Minecraft: build it your way!
- Minecraft: be here now!
- If you build it, creepers will come!
- Minecraft: nothing ventured, nothing gamed.
- The only thing we have to fear are creepers and other hostile mobs!

MINECRAFT SAYINGS WE'D LIKE TO SEE

- You don't know what you can do until you start building.
- The cavern you choose to enter may be filled with lava!
- Do no harm, unless you encounter creepers and other hostile mobs!
- No regrets, because you can respawn!
- Never underestimate the power of your Mine . . . craft!
- If you think it, you can build it.
- Minecraft: yes, you can!
- I see Herobrine!
- Minecraft: I'll be back!
- May the blocks be with you!
- Minecraft: to the Nether and beyond!
- I have a feeling we're not in the Nether anymore!
- Minecraft: another block in the wall!
- In the end, you know it's all blocks.
- "Mr. Steve, tear down this wall!"
- Gravity is a lifestyle choice.

- It's a big world. Someone has to explore it!
- I mine, therefore I craft!
- One player's hut is another player's castle!
- There's no place like the mines!
- Minecraft: doing the same thing over and over again and expecting different results.
- The best things in life are blocks.
- Be the miner and shape the world!
- Those who matter mine, and those who mine matter!
- When life gives you creepers . . . run!
- Keep calm and mine!
- Minecraft the Movie, Episode 1: The Dark Mine Rises!
- Minecraft the Movie, Episode 2: A Good Day to Mine Hard!
- I'm one step closer to diamonds!
- How to train your Ender Dragon!
- Minecraft the Movie, Episode 3: The Iron Golem Giant!
- Minecraft the Movie, Episode 4: Wreck-it Steve!

- Mine, create, survive!
- Minecraft: building a better world today and tomorrow!
- We are here to create!
- Don't mess with the creeper!
- Those diamonds won't mine themselves!
- Miners don't die—they respawn.
- Powered by Redstone!
- A diamond in your hand is worth two in a lava pool!
- Minecraft: so many blocks, so little time!
- When one portal closes, another one opens!
- If a creeper is in range, then so are you!
- "I'm not retreating! I'm advancing in another direction!"
- Minecraft: from the ground up!
- Don't just build it, create!
- May the Minecraft be with you!
- And another mob bites the dust!
- Be in Creative mode, play in adventure!

HILARIOUS JOKES FOR MINECRAFTERS

CHAPTER 1

HOSTILE MOBS

JOKES

Q: What happens when a creeper walks into a bar?

A: Everyone dies.

■

Q: Did you hear that the creeper was the life of the party?

A: He had a blast.

■

Q: What popular TV show do ghasts like to watch?

A: *Mobern Family*!

■

Q: Why can Minecraft spiders swim?

A: Because they have webbed feet!

Q: What do you get when you cross an Enderman with a creeper?

A: A teleporting bomb.

Q: What do Minecraft skeletons say before they sit down to dine?

A: "Bone appetite!"

■

Q: Why didn't the skeleton dance at the villagers' ball?

A: He had no body to dance with.

■

Q: How did Steve know that the skeleton was lying to him?

A: He could see right through him.

Q: What song does a blaze like to dance to?
A: "We Didn't Start the Fire."

■

Q: How do hostile mobs start a fairy tale?
A: "Once upon a slime . . ."

■

When I saw the witch with a potion, I knew trouble was brewing.

■

The Wither was confused and didn't know wither he should go to the Nether or not.

■

First zombie to a second zombie: "I'd tell you a joke about the end, but it will just dragon."

■

Q: Why did the creeper cross the road?
A: To escape the ocelot.

■

Q: Why did the Enderman stop playing?
A: Because he was at the end of his game.

Q: Why are there no posters of Endermen in Minecraft?
A: Because no one can look at them.

■

Q: How did the witch kill the player?
A: Her potions just blew him away.

■

Q: Why are Minecraft spiders always angry?
A: Because they keep going up the wall!

■

Q: What did the player say to the slime that he hadn't seen in a while?
A: "You gruesome."

■

Q: Why did the zombie cross the road?
A: To get to the next village.

■

Q: What do mosquitoes and zombies have in common?
A: They like a bite before bedtime!

Q: What kind of parties do creepers have?
A: Block parties.

■

Q: Why can't Endermen read an entire book?
A: Because they always start at the end.

■

Q: What games do zombies play with ants?
A: Squash.

■

Q: What do you say when you meet a Wither?
A: "Bye, Bye, Bye."

■

Q: What's a creeper's favorite toy?
A: A BOOM-a-rang.

■

Q: What do annoyed skeletons call noobs?
A: Blockheads.

Q: What's black and white and rolls off a pier?

A: An Enderman and a chicken fighting over a piece of cooked pork!

■

Q: Why do players shop at Endermen yard sales?

A: To get their stuff back.

■

Q: Why did the Enderman cross the road?

A: He didn't—he teleported.

■

Q: Where does an Enderman sleep?

A: Anywhere he wants.

■

Q: What did the zombie say to his friend who was up playing Minecraft all night?

A: "You look dead tired."

■

Q: What did the creeper call his tired silverfish?

A: A sleepy creepy!

Q: What goes "snap, crackle, pop"?

A: Silverfish in lava.

■

Q: What did one slime say to the other who hit him over the head?

A: "I'll get you next slime!"

Q: What did the zombie say to the new player?

A: "Pleased to eat you."

■

Q: Why did the slime stay home?

A: He had no place to goo!

Q: Why did the silverfish ground his children?
A: Because they were bugging him!

■

Q: Why did the zombie knit an extra sweater?
A: Because he wanted to keep his new family member warm.

■

Q: What did the creeper say to the player?
A: "Open the door, or I'll open the wall!"

■

Q: What do you get when you cross a chicken with a creeper?
A: The Grim Peeper.

■

Q: Why was the zombie happy to be in night court?
A: He was hoping the judge would grant him a new life sentence.

■

Q: What did the zombie say to his date?
A: "I've been dying to meet you."

Q: What do you get when a witch flies a plane?
A: A horror-flying experience.

■

Q: What do you call diamonds given to a creeper in exchange for a favor?
A: A monster bribe.

■

Q: What mobs slow down computers?
A: Rendermen!

■

Q: What's creepy and leads to the second floor of a creeper's house?
A: Monstairs.

■

Q: Where do zombies go hiking?
A: Death Valley.

■

Q: How do creepers like their eggs?
A: Terror fried.

Q: Why did the police hold the creeper after he was hit by lightning?

A: Because the creeper was charged!

■

Q: Why did the zombie leave the restaurant?

A: Because they weren't serving human beans, pickled kids, or eyes scream.

■

Q: Why did the zombie cross the road?

A: To get to the graveyard.

■

Q: Who are the heaviest creatures in Minecraft?

A: Skele-tons!

■

Q: Why does the zombie like ice cream?

A: Because while he's eating you, you scream.

■

Q: Why are creepers tired at the end of the day?

A: Because being evil is hard work.

Q: What type of contests do Endermen hate?
A: Staring contests!

■

Q: What did the mutant creeper say to the mutant Enderman?
A: "Stop sucking me in."

■

Did you know that Endermen scare people out of their mines?

■

Q: Why did the Enderman leave the party?
A: He felt uncomfortable with everyone staring at him.

■

Q: What did the creeper say to the noob?
A: "We hope you enjoy your ssstay."

■

The creeper is always greener on the other side.

■

Q: How many creepers does it take to blow up a lightbulb?
A: Just one! *Kaboom!*

Knock, knock.
Who's there?
Interrupting creeper.
Interrupting creep—
BOOM!

■

Q: What did the mom Enderman say to her child while he was getting dressed?
A: "Don't forget to wear clean *Enderwear*."

■

Q: What did the pig say to the creeper?
A: Nothing. The creeper blew up the pig.

■

Q: What do you call a blown-up creeper?
A: Dead.

■

Q: Why didn't the skeleton cross the road?
A: He didn't have enough guts.

Q: How do zombies and skeletons keep from burning during the day?
A: They stand on soul sand.

■

Q: How is a skeleton like a zombie?
A: They both spawn in darkness and burn in sunlight.

■

Knock, knock.
Who's there?
Creeper.
Creeper who?
Boom!

■

Two creepers walked into a bar. It took months to rebuild.

■

Q: How do you make a creeper destroy himself?
A: Give him a mirror.

First player: "I found a skeleton with a gold medal around his neck."
Second player: "What was on the medal?"
First player: "Minecraft Hide and Seek Champion 2009."

■

Q: Where do zombies like to hang out?
A: In the dead zone!

■

Q: Why was the zombie mad?
A: Because he couldn't get good TV reception when *The Walking Dead* was on!

■

If a creeper blows up in a forest and there is no one there to hear it, did he really make a boom?

If a creeper blows up in the forest and no one is there to see it, does anyone care?

■

Q: What did one creeper say to another other who kept on changing directions?
A: "Make up your mine!"

■

Q: What did the creeper say to the volcano?
A: "I lava you."

■

Q: What did the witch get by mixing a potion of spiders and rabbits?
A: Bugs Bunnies.

■

Q: What did the player say when he saw the creeper?
A: "Here comes the—*BOOM!*"

■

Q: What did the player say when he saw the creeper?
A: "Oh, BLAST!"

Q: What did the young creeper say to his parents before the party?
A: "This is going to be a BLAST!"

■

Q: Why did the witch couple get divorced?
A: They were driving each other batty.

■

Q: What did the young zombie say to his parents when he broke the vase?
A: "Oh, I'm so undead!"

■

Q: What do you call an Enderman on a diet?
A: A slenderman.

■

Q: Why is the creeper so awesome?
A: Because he blew my mind.

■

Q: What do you call a skeleton in an ice biome?
A: A numbskull.

Q: Why did the zombie run away from the player?
A: Because he was playing with fire.

■

Q: What do you call a group of zombies?
A: Mobsters.

■

Q: Two Minecraft zombies were fighting. Which one came out alive?
A: Neither. They're both dead.

■

Q: What did the zombie say when she broke up with her zombie boyfriend?
A: "You're dead to me."

■

Q: What does a vegan Minecraft zombie eat?
A: Raw potatoes, mushrooms, and grains.

■

Q: What is a zombie's favorite TV show?
A: *The Walking Dead*.

Q: What did the noob say to the zombie?
A: Nothing. The zombie killed the noob.

■

Q: What is a skeleton's favorite song?
A: "Can't Torch This!"

■

Q: What do Endermen hate more than being stared at?
A: Mirrors.

■

Q: What do you call an Enderman who spends all of his time at the gym?
A: A pumped up slenderman!

■

Q: Who went into a witch's hut and came out alive?
A: The witch.

■

Q: What goes "cackle, cackle, boom"?
A: A witch who mixes TNT with a bad potion.

Q: Why wasn't it a big deal when the zombie blew up his own stove?

A: Because zombies prefer raw food.

■

Q: What do you get if you cross a witch with a snow block?

A: A cold spell.

■

Q: What's the difference between a musician and a zombie?

A: One composes and the other decomposes.

■

Q: Why did the skeleton stay indoors on the sunny day?

A: He wanted to avoid sunburn.

■

Q: How do you make a creeper smile?

A: Turn him upside down.

■

Q: What did the zombie say to the Minecraft player?

A: "I love you for your brains."

Q: What did the zombie mob say to the noob?
A: "We're dying to have you for dinner."

■

Q: What do zombies say to Minecraft players?
A: "We're dying to meet you."

■

Q: Where do zombies go on vacation?
A: The Dead Sea.

■

Q: Where did the zombie build his house?
A: On a dead-end street.

■

Q: What part of your house do zombies avoid?
A: Your living room.

■

Q: What did the zombie ask the new player?
A: "You want a piece of me?"

Q: Where do zombies like to go swimming?
A: The Dead Sea.

■

Q: What is a zombie's favorite meal?
A: A Steve-wich.

■

Q: What did the zombie say to the player?
A: "You're on tonight's menu."

■

Q: How did you know that the zombie was sleepy?
A: He was dead on his feet.

■

First player: "Eww, there's a small slime in my apple."
Second player: "Hold on, I can get you a bigger one!"

Q: Why did the zombie cross the road?
A: To eat you.

■

First zombie: "How did you become a zombie?"
Second zombie: "It took *dead*ication."

■

Q: How nice was the zombie to the new player?
A: Very—he kept buttering her up.

■

Q: What did the zombie say when the player dug way, way down?
A: "It's mine, mine."

■

Q: Why did the Minecraft player keep on calling the skeleton "Napoleon"?
A: Because he was determined to make him Bone-a-part.

■

Q: What happened to the creeper when he failed to sneak up on a player?
A: He blew his chance!

Q: What kind of crackers do creepers like?
A: Firecrackers!

■

Q: How many zombies does it take to change a torch?
A: None. Zombies prefer darkness.

■

Q: Why did the player get mad at the creeper?
A: Because the creeper was trying to blow him up even though the player was just mining his own business.

■

The creeper got a job at an explosives factory. The next day, he got fired.

■

Q: What did the witch say when her potion exploded?
A: "I guess the whole thing blew up in my face."

■

Two zombies are eating a clown and one says to the other, "Does this taste funny to you?"

Two zombies were sitting at the dinner table when one turned to the other and said, "I hate eating Steve." The other replied, "So try the raw potatoes."

■

Q: What kind of food do zombies refuse to eat?
A: Lifesavers.

■

Q: Why didn't the dog come when Steve called?
A: Because the zombie bit his legs off.

■

Q: In addition to blocks, how do zombies keep others out of their houses?
A: They install dead bolts.

■

Q: Do zombies eat popcorn with their fingers?
A: No, they eat their fingers separately.

■

Q: What's a zombie's favorite bean?
A: A human bean.

Q: Why did the zombie with one hand cross the road?

A: To get to the second-hand shop!

■

Q: Why did the zombie wait to eat the creeper?

A: He had to wait for the green creeper to ripen.

■

Q: Why are Withers forgetful?

A: Because it goes in one ear and out the other.

■

Q: Why do Withers easily forget things?

A: Because everything goes in one head and not in the other two.

■

Q: Which mobs serve the best drinks in Minecraft?

A: Bartendermen!

■

Q: How did the creeper plant the roses?

A: He blew them up.

TONGUE TWISTERS

Which Witch Won With Which Weapon?

Charged Creepers Carry Crafty Crazy Combustible Explosions.

Creepers Chase Courageous Kids.

Which Witch Was Wicked?

Charged Creepers Colliding Cause Creepers to Crumble!

A Skeleton's Sword Slays Skeletons!

Black Back Bats.

Black Batty Bats.

MINECRAFT LIMERICKS, POEMS, AND HAIKUS

Nighttime in Minecraft has come.
The footsteps of zombies would drum.
They marched through the street,
Looking for something to eat.
Take care, or your life will succumb.

As I mined all night long, I went deeper.
I wouldn't stop and dug steeper.
Without sleep I felt brave
And entered a dark cave
And laughed in the face of a creeper.

■

I built a grand villa of rocks.
I used stone and obsidian blocks.
It stands thirty blocks tall.
Creepers try to climb the wall.
Frustrated, they pickaxe the locks.

■

I tried to give the zombie mushroom stew.
He shouted that stew wouldn't do.
"I'm vegan," I told him. "I don't eat meat."
He said he would start with my feet.
So out of the cave I flew.

■

I mine all night
With creepers who come out to fight.
I blow them up with TNT.
Goodness, this game is so much fun for me!

■

When zombies come out at night
They give us a scare and a big fright.
They wander biomes
And love to roam.
If you see one, run with all your might.

■

A zombie ate chickens undead.
And this is what he said:
"It clucked in my belly,
While I watched the telly,
And it clucked as I lay in my bed."

■

I spot a creeper.
He's in need of a big hug.
Closer he comes—BOOM!

■

We call them undead for a reason.
They've committed acts of treason.
Try to chop off their heads.
Watch out if they bled.
In Minecraft, it's zombie-hunting season.

■

There once was a creeper with a big frown.
A player tried in vain to turn it upside down.
When he came near,
The creeper showed no fear.
He blew up the player's town.

■

The player wasn't a leaper.
Instead he dug his pickaxe deeper.
He gave it a go,
And what do you know?
He landed on top of a creeper.

■

Creepers inspire
feelings of utter terror.
Run away quickly.

■

There once was a zombie named Zane.
He was incredibly insane.
His victim—a player—
Failed at defeating this slayer.
Now Zane is enjoying his brains!

■

The safest hideout is in a mall
That I built with locked doors and a thick wall.
Well, now I'm surrounded
And constantly hounded
By a zombie who won't take a fall.

■

There once was a zombie named Ed.
He certainly was quite undead.
He surprised me so
And bit off my toe.
I limp around now filled with dread.

DID YOU KNOW...?

Did you know that a skeleton will shoot itself if you are under or over it?

Did you know that zombies and skeletons won't burn during the day if they are standing on soul sand?

Did you know that creepers have four legs?

Did you know that Endermen have purple eyes?

Did you know that an Enderman's weakness is water?

Did you know that when you summon a Wither it will gain health, explode, and destroy everything?

CHAPTER 2

NETHER MOBS

JOKES

Q: Why don't blazes make good managers?
A: They keep firing people.

■

Q: What did the blaze get when he threw fire at a box of apples?
A: Baked apples.

■

Q: Why is Belgium filled with lava?
A: Because it is next to the Nether-lands.

■

Q: What did the blaze champion say to his opponent?
A: "I won fair and square."

Q: What type of streets do ghasts haunt?
A: Dead ends!

■

Q: Where do ghasts go on holiday?
A: The Nether-lands.

■

Q: Why can't blazes keep their jobs?
A: Because they are always getting fired.

■

Q: Why do ghasts shoot fireballs and not water?
A: Water evaporates.

Q: Why didn't the boat crash?
A: Because it landed on soul sand.

■

Q: What did the ghast say to the player in the Nether?
A: "You're *Nether* going to get out of here!"

■

Q: What did one slime say to the other slime?
A: "Do you mind if I stick with you?"

■

Q: What did one slime say to the other slime when he was leaving?
A: "Slime you later."

■

Q: What did the slime say when he quickly fell off a cliff?
A: "See how fast slime flies!"

■

Q: What do you get when you cross a pig with a blaze?
A: Pork chops.

Q: What do you get when you build a frame out of obsidian and light it with fire?
A: A Nether portal.

■

Q: What did the ghast say when he was stuck?
A: I will *Nether* get out of here.

■

Q: What animals do ghasts sound like?
A: High-pitched cats.

■

Q: What sounds closer than it actually is?
A: A ghast when it is destroying things.

■

Q: What is a ghast's favorite song?
A: "Great Balls of Fire."

■

Q: What's a ghast's favorite food?
A: Pumpkin pie with I-scream.

First player: "Who's the greatest Cubist of the twenty-first century?"
Second player: "Notch!"

■

Q: What did the ghast say when the zombie pigman started showing off?
A: "What a ham."

■

Q: Where does a baby ghast go when his parents are at work?
A: Dayscare.

■

Q: How did the player avoid being attacked by the zombie pigman?
A: He ignored him and *Nether* gave him a thought.

Q: Why did the zombie pigman cross the road?
A: Because he was riding a chicken.

■

Q: How did Peter Pan wind up in the Nether?
A: He took a wrong turn flying to Neverland!

■

Q: How do you get to a ghast's house?
A: Walk down the street until you reach the dead end.

■

Q: What does a ghast say when he's happy?
A: "I'm having a blast!"

■

Q: What does a ghast say when he's upset?
A: "How ghastly!"

■

Q: What did the grandfather ghast say to his grandson who he hadn't seen for a long time?
A: "Wow, you gruesome."

Q: Why was the ghast crying?
A: Everyone he liked blew up!

■

Q: What did the critic say about the ghast's artwork?
A: "It's a monsterpiece."

■

The bookstore owner said to a Wither, "Here's a good book to help you get ahead." The Wither answered, "No, thank you, I already have three heads!"

■

Q: What happened to the snow golem who entered the Nether?
A: He became a puddle.

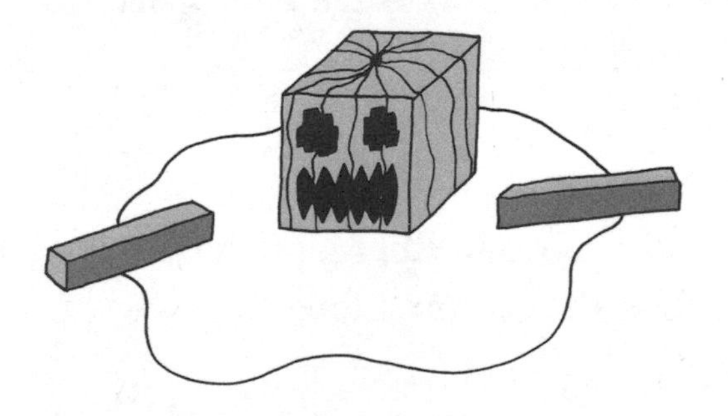

Q: What's the best way to speak to a ghast?
A: Long distance.

■

Q: Why are ghasts so miserable?
A: Because they find everything ghastly.

■

Q: What type of horses do ghasts ride?
A: Night mares.

■

Q: What is the national anthem of the Nether?
A: "Burn, Baby, Burn!"

■

Q: How did the players in the Nether feel the first time they saw the noob?
A: They were *a*-ghast.

■

Q: Why was the Minecraft player confused?
A: There were two shovels in a chest and he couldn't choose!

Q: Why did the noob leave the mines?
A: He was scared to death of the Nethers.

■

Q: Why are there no cars in Minecraft?
A: Because hostile mobs blocked all of the roads.

■

Q: Why did the bartender throw the baby ghast out of the bar?
A: Because he was a miner.

■

Q: How does a snake scare a ghast?
A: He yells, "Boa!"

■

Q: How did the player feel about the Nether portal?
A: It left him *a*-ghast.

■

Q: What's a blaze's favorite song?
A: "I'm on Fire."

Q: What song did the blaze like?
A: "Don't Play with Fire!"

■

Q: What song did the blaze mob play at the concert?
A: "Light My Fire."

■

Q: What dance song was the blaze dancing to?
A: "Jump into the Fire."

■

Q: What did the blaze say to the one he loves?
A: "I'm burnin' for you."

■

Q: How are slimes like rabbits?
A: They both hop.

■

Q: How did the Wither know that the three-headed monster was going to storm into the Nether?
A: He checked the *Wither* Channel.

Q: What can the smartest Minecraft players solve?

A: Rubik's Magma Cubes!

■

Q: What's a larger, scarier version of a skeleton?

A: A wither skeleton!

■

Q: What did the player do with the Nether wart?

A: He planted it, let it bloom, and used it for brewing potions.

■

Q: How did the player move long distances so quickly?

A: He used a portal in the Nether.

■

Q: How could you tell the zombie pigmen were tired?

A: They were dead on their feet.

TONGUE TWISTERS

Gargantuan Ghastly Ghasts Gather.

Nexus or Nether? Notch Knows.

Players Pass Purple Portals.

Firing Fiery Flaming Fireballs.

Nether Mind Nether Mobs for Nether Mobs don't Mind Miners.

Slimes Spawn in Swamps.

MINECRAFT LIMERICKS, POEMS, AND HAIKUS

Trying to get sleep?
Stay out of the bed, or else
Players will explode!

■

In the Nether you must beware!
Listen to this warning and take care!
Players stay out of beds.
For explosions will shatter your heads!

■

To get a blaze rod
Watch for hurling fireballs.
That the blaze will throw.

■

Duck, quick, be careful.
The blaze hurls large fireballs
Right at you, *kaboom!*

■

Ghasts drop gunpowder
Collect ghast tears when they die
Use them in potions

■

Make ghast-proof buildings.
Use stone from the Overworld.
Ha-ha! You've tricked them.

■

Should you be so bold
to let ghasts fire at you?
They light your portal.

■

Time spent playing Minecraft
Is anything but daft.
The possibilities broaden my scope
and fill me with lots of hope.
We insiders get the last laugh!

■

To me, Minecraft is more than a game.
To my parents, my obsession's quite insane.
Blowing up a ghast in the Nether.
Makes me feel better.
Anticipating my next move.
I am in the building groove.

■

The Withers shoot skulls
That look just like their own heads.
Watch out—they explode.

■

If you kill one and collect his head,
Hold on—it's code red.
More are on the rise.
A wither skeleton has hit you by surprise.
Your body withers, and now you're dead.

■

A mixed-up ghast named Jean
Was incredibly wicked and mean.
He chased me around,
And I fell on the ground.
Now Jean got hold of my spleen!

DID YOU KNOW...?

Did you know that there is no way to place water in the Nether? Even smashed or melted ice will not turn into water!

Did you know that you can avoid being hit by a ghast by blocking his line of sight with transparent blocks?

Did you know that killing magma cubes cause them to break and divide?

Did you know that skeletons have cousins in the Nether called wither skeletons?

Did you know that the Wither boss will kill any mob?

Did you know that the wither skeleton can poison you with a potion effect that leeches life away when it hits you?

Did you know that magma cubes are a cousin of Overworld slimes?

Did you know that if you attack just one zombie pigman, all zombie pigmen will also attack?

Did you know that zombie pigmen only spawn in the Nether?

Did you know that zombie pigmen keep on attacking even if you are dead?

CHAPTER 3

GUARDIANS AND VILLAGERS

JOKES

Elder guardian: "What's the main difference between LEGO and Minecraft?"
Ocean guardian: "With LEGO, you don't die."

■

Q: What can be heard up to one hundred blocks away?
A: A guardian's laser sound.

■

Q: What happens when blocks break in the ocean?
A: They get wet!

Q: What type of guardian sits on the bottom of the ocean and shakes?

A: A nervous wreck.

■

Q. When elder guardians look back on life, what do they miss the most?

A. Blowing things up!

■

Q: Why did the elder guardian feel ill?

A: His nose was blocked up.

Q: What did the villager say to the other villager?
A: Nothing, because villagers don't talk.

■

Q: What's another name for a villager's hut?
A: A panic room.

■

Q: Which zombie villager won the battle?
A: It was a dead-tie!

■

Q: What did the villagers get when they divided the circumference of a pumpkin by its diameter?
A: Pumpkin pi!

■

Q: Why did the villager fail math?
A: He had a mental block.

■

Q: How did one villager inspire the new Minecraft player?
A: He told him that the world is his Minecraft and he can build anything!

Q: Why did the villagers hold the iron golem over a fire pit?

A: To get the wrinkles out of their clothing.

■

Q: Why are villagers antisocial?

A: They keep saying "Mine, mine, mine."

■

Q: What song do villagers like to hum?

A: "We Built This City."

■

Q: What's a villager's favorite show tune?

A: "It's a Hard-block Life."

■

Q: What did the villagers sing when the Endermen cornered them?

A: "Trapped."

■

Q: Why did the player get a stomachache?

A: He ate too much creepy pasta!

Q: How do crazy villagers go through the forest?
A: They take the psychopath!

■

First villager: "What do you call small slime?"
Second villager: "Slim!"

■

Q: What did the villager-turned-DJ do at the party?
A: He turned the music up a Notch.

■

Q: What did one villager say to the other?
A: "A-u, give me back my gold!"

■

Q: How do creepers play music?
A: On their BOOM boxes.

Q: How can you tell if a villager is in love?
A: He walks very slowly.

■

Q: Why did the zombie villager turn purple and get nauseous for ten seconds?
A: He was cured!

■

Q: Why couldn't anyone tell the two zombie villagers apart?
A: They were dead-ringers!

■

Q: Why did the zombie villager go crazy?
A: Because he lost his mind!

■

First villager: "How many Minecraft players does it take to screw in a lightbulb?"
Second villager: "None. Players use torches."

■

Q: Why was the eighth villager crying on his birthday?
A: Because he had seven guests at his party and it takes seven bites to eat a cake!

Q: Why did the villagers think the skeleton wouldn't attack them?

A: Because the skeleton didn't have any guts.

■

Q: What did one hippie villager say to the other hippie villager?

A: "Hey, man, can you dig it?"

■

Q: What did one villager say to his friend when another villager was rude?

A: "Nether mind him."

■

Q: Why do hip villagers hate Minecraft?

A: Because it's full of squares!

■

First villager: "How do you know when your friends are playing too much Minecraft?"

Second villager: "Just shout 'creeper' and watch everyone dive under their desks."

Q: What has a dog's head and a kitten's tail?

A: A zombie villager coming out of a pet store.

■

Q: Why was the zombie villager off his game?

A: Because he was dead tired!

■

Q: What food would you never see a zombie villager eating?

A: Lifesavers!

■

Q: What room should you build to keep out zombie villagers?

A: A living room!

TONGUE TWISTERS

Billy Bob Built Buildings by Breaking Boulders.

Great Green Guardians Growl.

Groups of Guardians Guard Gracefully.

Elders Eyes Emit Eerie Effects.

Guardians Guarding Gilttery Gold.

Prized Pretty Prismarine.

Trade Trinkets Trade Tools.

Surly Swarms Stinging Strongly.

Minding Manners Matter Most in the Mines.

MINECRAFT LIMERICKS, POEMS, AND HAIKUS

Guardians attack
By sending out laser beams.
Careful, they can kill.

■

Guardians target
And harm players in water.
Avoid the water.

Guardians swim well
Searching for players and squid.
Boats won't keep you safe.

■

Falling to their death.
It takes thirty-two long blocks.
Guardian goes splat.

■

Elder guardians
Spawn in ocean monuments
And are hostile mobs.

■

Elder guardians
Attack firing lasers
And cause mine fatigue.

■

Beware of Elders.
These guardians cause much pain
With thorn-like attacks.

■

Elder guardians
Will drop prismarine crystals
If raw fish drop fails.

■

Elder guardians
Are sometimes spawned through commands
And don't have spawn eggs.

■

I play Minecraft all day and all night.
It gives the villagers a bit of a fright.
They worry that the only sunlight I see
Is the one in the biome with me.

■

Don't leave, villager.
Leaving means you won't return.
You'll be greatly missed.

■

No x-ray vision.
Invisible? We see you!
So don't try to hide.

■

An invisibility potion won't protect
From guardians; it has no effect.
They hope that their ink
Will cause them to sink.
But guardians use their powers to detect.

DID YOU KNOW...?

Did you know that villager children like to play tag?

Did you know that creepy pasta are internet scary stories told in forums and other sites?

Did you know that villagers were once called testificates and that they are intelligent and passive?

Did you know you can cure zombie villagers if you throw a splash potion on them and feed them golden apples?

Did you know that villagers resemble a cavemen Squidward?

Did you know that 5 percent of all zombies are zombie villagers?

Did you know that zombie villagers behave just like ordinary zombies except their heads and face look like villagers with a darker green color?

CHAPTER 4

PASSIVE AND TAMABLE MOBS

JOKES

Q: What happened to the sheep that stepped on a flower?
A: It dyed.

■

Q: Why did the chicken cross the web?
A: To get to the other site.

■

Q: What did one cow say to the other in the tiny hut?
A: "There isn't *mush*room in here!"

■

Q: What happened to the sheep named Jeb?
A: Its wool faded between all the sheep colors.

Q: What do you get when you cross a cow with a mushroom?

A: A mooshroom.

Knock, knock.

Who's there?

Interrupting mooshroom.

Interrupting m—

Moooo!

■

Q: Did you hear about the cow that tried to escape over a barbed wire fence?

A: Yes! It was an udder disaster.

Q: What did the cow say to the angry mob?
A: "Moo!"

■

Q: What happened when a large herd of cows was destroyed?
A: It was udder annihilation.

First player: "What a cute bunch of cows on that farm."
Second player: "It's a herd."
First player: "Heard of what?"
Second player: "Herd of cows."
First player: "Of course, I've heard of cows!"

■

Q: Why was the cow broke?
A: Because the players milked it dry.

■

Q: Did you hear about the kitten that ate the sheep?
A: She had mittens!

Q: What do you get when you cross a chicken with a male kitten?

A: A peeping tom.

■

Q: Why is it so hard for ocelots to hide in Minecraft?

A: Because they are always spotted.

■

Q: Why did the cow cross the road?

A: To get to the udder side.

■

Q: Why are some Minecraft cows musical?

A: They make a sound like a kazoo!

■

Q: How do wolves eat rotten flesh and raw chickens?

A: They wolf them down.

■

Q: Why did the chicken cross the road?

A: He was following the player carrying seeds.

Q: Why did the player cry wolf?
A: He was looking for his dog!

■

Q: Why did the tamed cats go wild?
A: The player forgot to feed them for two days!

■

Q: Why did the player ride his horse across the road?
A: It was too heavy to carry!

■

Q: Can horses jump higher than a house in Minecraft?
A: Of course! Houses can't jump!

■

Q: What do you call a horse that neighs and whinnies?
A: A herd animal.

■

Q: What did the player say when he fell off the horse?
A: "I've fallen and can't giddyup!"

Q: What do you call noisy horses that live in the next biome?
A: "Neigh-bors."

■

Q: When do Minecraft horses talk?
A: Whinney wants to!

■

Q: When does a sheep sound like a cheerleader?
A: When a creeper blows him up. He goes "baaah boom baaah!"

■

Q: How many sheep does it take to knit a sweater?
A: None. Minecraft sheep don't knit.

■

Q: Why do so many pigs die in Minecraft?
A: Because there are no *h*ambulances.

■

Q: What did the player say after he blew up the sheep?
A: *Baaaaah boom!*

Q: What do you call a sheep with TNT?

A: A *baaaad* situation.

■

Q: Why did the cow cross the road?

A: She was following the Minecraft player carrying wheat.

■

Q: What happens if your cat dies?

A: It's a cat-astrophy!

■

Q: Did you hear the one about the cat who was an ocelot?

A: She was purr-plexed.

■

Q: Why did the cat cross several blocks?

A: To be with her player!

Q: Why did the Minecraft player love her ocelot kitten?
A: Because she was purr-fect!

■

Q: Why did the player call his dog Frost?
A: Because Frost bites!

■

Q: How do you know that all Minecraft cows are female?
A: Because all cows in Minecraft give milk.

■

Q: What do players say about Minecraft cows?
A: They should been seen and not herd!

■

Q: What do you call a coffee-colored cow that just gave birth?
A: De-*calf*enated.

Q: What type of room was the Minecraft player building for the cow?

A: A calf-ateria.

■

Q: Where was the rabbit when the lights went out?

A: In the dark.

■

Q: What type of books do Minecraft rabbits like to read?

A: Ones with jokes and hoppy endings.

■

There were two cows in a field. One mooed. The other said, "I was going to say that!"

■

Q: Why doesn't Sweden import cattle?

A: Because they have good Stockholm!

■

Q: Why did the cow cross the road?

A: He didn't want to be creamed by the player!

Q: What goes *oom oom*?
A: A cow walking backwards on a Minecraft road.

■

Q: What can you find between Pigzilla's toes?
A: Small runners.

■

Q: What does Pigzilla eat at the all-you-can-eat restaurant?
A: "Anything he wants."

■

Q: What Minecraft character is Kermit the Frog afraid of?
A: Pigzilla!

■

Q: Why should you never share your secrets with a pig?
A: Because they always squeal.

■

Q: Why can't you mix chickens with TNT?
A: They might eggs-plode.

■

If a Minecraft cow laughed, would milk come out of its nose?

Q: How do you make a Minecraft squid laugh?
A: Tickle him six times.

■

Q: In what part of Minecraft do you find a down-and-out squid?
A: On Squid Row.

■

First player: "Would you rather a giant squid attack you or a creeper?"
Second player: "I'd rather the giant squid attack the creeper."

■

Q: What famous pirate sails the open seas in Minecraft?
A: Captain Squid.

■

Q: What do you call a pig that takes up two lanes on the highway?
A: A road hog.

■

Q: What did the player say to the bat?
A: "I'm going to bat-tle you."

Q: Why did the pig jump in the water?

A: Because the player said, "Hogwash."

■

Q: Why should you be quiet around sheep?

A: Because they are ashleep!

■

Q: What do you call a sheep after a mob blows off its legs?

A: A cloud.

■

Q: What happened to the strange-colored sheep?

A: It dyed.

■

Q: How did the sheep change directions?

A: It made a ewe-turn.

■

Q: What did the pig say to the player who caught it by its tail?

A: "That's the end of me."

Q: Why did the pig cross the road?
A: Because it was the chicken's day off.

■

Q: Why do chicken coops have two doors?
A: Because if they had four, they'd be chicken sedans and we all know there are no cars in Minecraft!

■

The talented pig learned karate. Now he's dropping pork chops.

■

Q: What do you call Batman and Robin after they are trampled by Pigzilla?
A: Flatman and Ribbon.

■

Q: What happened to the pig that was struck by lightning?
A: He turned into zombie pigman!

■

Q: How did the player die from drinking milk?
A: The cow fell on him.

Q: Why did the squid cross the road?
A: To get to the other tide.

■

Q: What do you get when you pour hot lava down a rabbit hole?
A: Hot cross bunnies.

■

Q: How did the Scottish puppy feel when he saw a Wither?
A: Terrierfied.

■

Q: Why did the puppy cross the road?
A: To get to the barking lot.

■

Q: What do Minecraft players feed puppies for breakfast?
A: Pooched eggs.

■

Q: What do you call a row of rabbits that hops backwards?
A: A receding hare line.

Q: Why did the wolf cross the road?

A: He was chasing the player.

■

Q: What do you get when you cross a puppy with a calculator?

A: A dog you can count on!

■

Q: Why do Minecraft horses eat golden apples and golden carrots with their mouths open?

A: Because they have no stable manners!

■

Q: What do you call a frozen puppy in a polar biome?

A: A pupsicle!

■

Q: What did the skeleton say to the puppy?

A: "Bone appetite!"

Q: How do you turn a rabbit into toast?

A. Name him "Toast" by using a name tag or a renamed spawn egg.

■

Q: Why did the wolves cross the road?

A: The sheep were on the other side.

Q: Why did the chicken run away?

A: Because he heard the player calling fowls.

■

Knock, knock!

Who's there?

Chicken.

Chicken who?

Just chicken out your door!

■

Q: What did the player say after his sheep were blown up?

A: "Oh where, oh where, have my little sheep gone?"

TONGUE TWISTERS

Mining Minecraft Mines Make Me Merry.

Sheeps Shun Selfies.

Sheeps Say Sheariously!

Seriously Sheared Sheep.

Cows Cross Across Coarse Courses.

Colorful Cows Climb Craggy Cliffs.

Parents Protect Piglets.

Players Picked Pink Pigs.

Squash a Squirming Stepped-on Squid.

Rapid Rabid Rabbit.

Wolves Watch Witches While Witches Watch Wolves.

Chomping Chirping Chickens Chatter.

MINECRAFT LIMERICKS, POEMS, AND HAIKUS

Flying unaware
Into very hot lava.
We catch on fire.

■

We sleep all day long.
And if you're invisible,
We can still see you.

■

The sheep is called Jeb.
Prism colored fluffy wool.
He shimmers all night.

■

A sheep eats grass blocks,
Which turn into piles of dirt.
And their wool grows back.

■

Tamed wolves will attack
Skeletons if unprovoked.
They're wanting the bones!

■

Teleporting wolves
Visit owners far away
In twelve blocks or more.

■

When you spot a horse,
If untamed, don't saddle him.
He will flail his hooves.

■

He whinnies and neighs.
Donkeys and mules emit brays.
Tamed horses move fast.

■

Riders are thrown off.
If your horse is in water,
It's hard to remount.

■

Skeleton horses
Sound just like normal horses.
They're made up of bones.

■

Horses can be bred.
Just feed them golden apples.
Soon babies appear.

■

Want a baby mule?
Just mate a donkey and horse.
Isn't he quite cute!

■

Ocelot kittens
Found randomly are quite fast
And are hard to catch.

■

To breed a tamed cat
Give him raw fish to enjoy.
Soon you'll have kittens.

■

Growing up too fast.
Your baby cat keeps growing.
Feed him uncooked fish.

■

Tamed cats are loyal
And will follow you around.
They purr frequently.

■

We're active night.
And hang upside down on blocks.
Lava will burn us.

A black-and-white kitten named Spot
Caused trouble all day, quite a lot.
He fell down the stairs,
Scratched all of the chairs,
And loved the attention he got.

Covered in sacs of ink.
From head to toe, I think.
I killed a passive squid,
And this I do not kid,
I just wish the ink were pink!

Squids move up and down
Using their tentacles to push them around
As they move away from the light.
They prefer darkness more than things that are bright.
And always remain passive in town.

■

Give two cows some wheat.
They will quickly fall in love
And make baby calves.

■

Minecraft cows in a happy *moood.*
It's wheat they fancy, their favorite food.
If they eat this, tiny calves will appear
And will draw players near
As they watch the cows being wooed.

■

Rabbits hop around.
Carrots and dandelions
Are their favorites.

■

Rabbits love carrots.
To reach them, they'll jump off cliffs,
Avoiding lava.

■

Rabbits grow up fast.
After just twenty minutes,
They become adults.

■

The killer bunny
Is faster than a rabbit
And has blood red eyes.

■

Killer bunnies hop
Much like a spider—he's fast.
Careful, he will lunge.

■

Wheat seeds breed chickens.
They produce cute baby chicks
That grow up quite fast.

■

It takes just seconds
For baby chickens to grow.
Just feed them wheat seeds.

■

Want to spawn chickens?
You have a one-in-eight chance
If you throw an egg.

■

Bats sleep all day and are active at night.
If you approach, they'll take flight.
Invisible players, they can see you!
No harm, no fear, for this is true!
Flying into lava is their demise.
And you may hear their high-pitched cries!

■

A scrawny little bat named Clark
flew up from bedrock, which was dark.
He grew big wings that were scary.
They almost looked shaggy and hairy,
so his bite wasn't worse than his bark!

■

When falling from high above
A chicken flaps its wings like a dove.
This makes them immune to being smashed
As they avoid getting crashed.
So don't give a chicken a shove!

■

Players be aware:
Stay away from untamed wolves
Spawned naturally.

■

Wild wolves, with gray hair
And long drooping fluffy tails,
Harm rabbits and sheep.

■

Distinguished by their constant growling,
It doesn't sound like howling.
The wolf's tail becomes straight.
He is looking for bait.
A hostile wolf will leave you scowling.

■

Pigs act passively.
They avoid falling off cliffs.
And they eat carrots.

■

Show him a carrot.
He will always follow you.
Sometimes he will oink.

■

The giant pig means no harm.
He'd be better off on a farm.
Knocking over everything in his path.
I try really hard not to laugh.

■

There was an old wolf whose habits
Induced him to feed upon rabbits.
When he'd eaten eighteen,
He turned perfectly green
And kept on saying, "Dagnabbit!"

■

There once was a sheep with no hair.
He felt cold and oh so bare.
He was sheared down to his toes
And right up to his nose.
Alas, that poor sheep felt despair.

DID YOU KNOW...?

Did you know that squids spawn at sea level?

Do dogs in Minecraft run in circles or in squares?

Did you know that Minecraft rabbits have such good eyesight that they can see food from a farther distance than any other mob?

Did you know that the name of the "Killer Rabbit of Caerbannog" is a tribute to the rabbit in the movie *Monty Python and the Holy Grail*?

Did you know that the Killer Rabbit of Caerbannog runs faster than normal rabbits?

Did you know that "Toast" is the name of a rabbit that was added as a tribute to a player who lost his own rabbit?

Did you know that shearing a mooshroom drops five red mushrooms and turning it into a normal cow?

Did you know that to lure a pig you must put a carrot on a fishing rod?

Did you know that you can tame ocelots by giving them raw fish?

Did you know that you can tame wolves by feeding them bones?

CHAPTER 5

SNOW AND IRON GOLEMS

JOKES

Q: Did you hear about the snow golem's murder?
A: It's a cold case.

■

Q: What happened to the snow golem who got bit by a wolf?
A: He got frostbite.

■

Q: What do you get when you cross a snow golem with a zombie?
A: Frostbite.

■

Q: What do snow golems love to put on their food?
A: Chili sauce!

Q: What happened when it became so cold in the icy biome?

A: The snow golems were holding up pictures of thumbs!

■

Q: What do you call a snow golem on rollerblades?

A: A snowmobile.

■

Q: What do you call snow golems that visit the Nether?

A: Snowballs!

■

Q: Why do snow golems often look like they are dressed for Halloween?

A: Because they wear pumpkins as helmets.

■

Q: How do you make an infinite amount of snow?

A: Trap a snow golem in a 1x1 hole and dig the snow away from under his feet.

■

Q: What would a snow golem's favorite breakfast food be?

A: Frosted Flakes.

Q: Why didn't the snow golem spawn?
A: Because he was in a snow biome.

■

Q: They are not weightless in water and despite their name they can't drown. What are they?
A: Iron golems.

■

First snow golem: "Knock, knock!"
Second snow golem: "Who's there?"
First snow golem: "Snow."
Second snow golem: "Snow who?"
First snow golem: "It's *snow* laughing matter."

■

Q: What do you call a dead snow golem?
A: Water.

■

Q: What did one snow golem say to the other?
A: "Ice to meet you!"

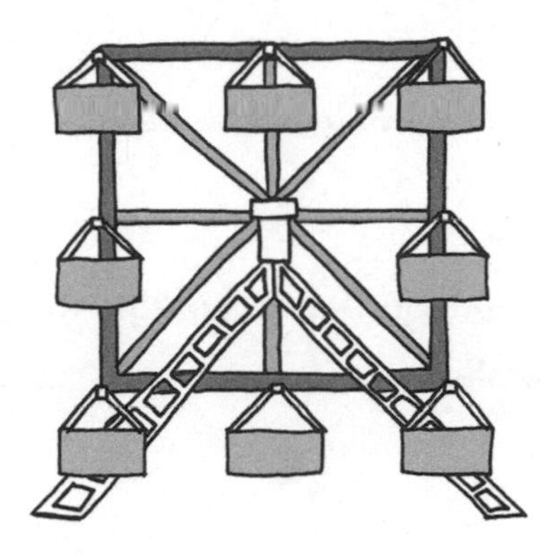

Q: Why was the iron golem sad?

A: Because the player couldn't create a round Ferris wheel.

■

Q: Why did the snow golem break up with her boyfriend?

A: Because she thought he was a flake.

■

Q: Why don't iron golems like to swim?

A: Because they rust.

■

Q: What do you get when a blaze and a snow golem meet?

A: A puddle.

Q: Why don't other mobs invite snow golems to a sauna?
A: Because they're big drips.

■

Q: What did the snow golem say to his psychiatrist?
A: "I feel abominable."

■

Q: What did the iron golem say to the player who was about to be destroyed?
A: "I'll granite you one last wish!"

■

Q: Why did everyone like the iron golem after he was struck by lightning?
A: Because he developed a magnetic personality!

■

Q: What kind of math do snow golems teach their owls?
A: Owlgebra.

■

Q: Where do snow golems keep their money?
A: In snowbanks.

Q: What happened to the snow golem that hugged a blaze?
A: He turned into a puddle of water.

■

Q: What happened to the snow golem that high-fived a blaze?
A: He melted.

■

Q: What happened to the snow golem that slapped a blaze?
A: He was destroyed.

■

Q: What do snow golems call their kids?
A: Chill-dren.

■

Q: What do you call a dead snow golem?
A: Water.

■

Q: What do you call an iron golem that does a cartwheel?
A: A ferrous wheel.

Q: What is an iron golem's favorite movie?
A: *Ferrous Bueller's Day Off.*

■

Q: If an iron golem and the silver surfer teamed up, what would you call them?
A: Alloys!

■

Q: How do snow golems make their beds?
A: With sheets of ice and blankets of snow.

■

Q: What do you call a snow golem in the desert?
A: A puddle.

■

Q: What happened to the snow golem who was stressed?
A: He had a meltdown!

■

Q: What do snow golems eat on very cold days?
A: *Sub-hero* sandwiches.

Q: What do snow golems wear on their heads?
A: Ice caps.

■

Q: What happens when two snow golems get into a fight?
A: They give each other the cold shoulder.

■

Q: Where do snow golems dance?
A: At a snowball.

■

Q: How do some snow golems travel?
A: On icicles.

■

Q: What happened to the iron golem who got bite by the snow golem?
A: He got frostbite.

■

Q: What do snow golems leave behind?
A: A trail of snow.

Q: Why did the Ender Dragon eat the iron golem?
A: Because he was anemic.

MINECRAFT LIMERICKS, POEMS, AND HAIKUS

The iron golem attacked quickly.
His victims, the mobs, were quite prickly.
They overpowered him.
He was feeling grim
Being wounded and acting quite sickly.

■

There once was a snow golem named Burt.
He wandered, got lost, and was hurt.
His figure, once svelte,
Had started to melt.
Now he's a puddle in the desert.

■

There once was a snow golem named Hannah.
She wore a bright yellow bandana.
One sunny day,
She melted away,
Because she made her way into a savanna.

■

There once was an iron golem named Bob.
His aim was perfected on mobs.
He hit each one well,
That all of them fell,
And his attackers became a big blob.

■

Patrolling the villages is their passion.
Being close to the edges of buildings is their fashion.
They don't wander far.
With villagers they will not spar.
Giving them poppies is how they show compassion.

■

Leaving trails of snow,
Snow golems carry winter
Almost everywhere.

Wanders aimlessly.
The snow golem throws snowballs
And angers the mob.

■

Passive snow golems
Drop snowballs upon their death.
Not pumpkins for you.

■

Rain, rain go away.
It's what snow golems would say,
Because rainfall hurts.

■

Place two blocks of snow
On top of one another
Then add a pumpkin.

■

With your snow body and pumpkin head,
Entering the Nether you'll soon be dead.
Throwing snowballs at angry mobs
Won't harm them or turn them into frogs.
Your best bet is to escape on a sled.

■

We're not related.
Don't hit me with a snowball.
Iron can kill snow.

■

They won't attack you unless you attack first.
It's the zombies they consider the worst.
Iron golems protect villagers from them.
It's zombies that they condemn.
So mind your own business or they will cause you to burst!

■

Avoiding lava is what iron golems do.
Lava will burn them, it's true.
Icy waters have no effect.
Yet, water they don't reject.
It's hot lava that they cannot pull through.

Don't you throw that snowball at me.
Don't chance it, for if you do, you will see.
I will get you with one quick throw.
You'll be covered in snow,
For snow golems can kill iron golems—so let it be.

DID YOU KNOW...?

Did you know that iron golems get mad if snow golems accidently hit them or hit villagers when aiming at other mobs?

Did you know that iron golems giving flowers to villager children is a reference to the ancient robots in Hayao Miyazaki's animated film *Castle in the Sky*?

Did you know that snow golems will not attack creepers?

Did you know that you need two blocks and one pumpkin to spawn a snow golem?

Did you know that snow golems can't kill slimes or magma cubes?

Did you know that villagers love iron golems because iron golems protect them?

Did you know that an iron golem needs ten doors and twenty-one houses to spawn?

Did you know that iron golems give baby villagers flowers?

Did you know that iron golems won't die if they fall—even from very high places?

Did you know that two iron golems can fight one another? They face each other, slowly back up, and then charge!

Did you know that snow golems die in the desert and in the Nether?

Did you know that snow golems are created from snow blocks and a pumpkin, and that iron golems are made from iron blocks and a pumpkin?

Did you know that if a snow golem hits a blaze with three snowballs, it will die?

CHAPTER 6

STEVE AND ALEX

JOKES

Q: What non-Minecraft character could Steve run into if he dug all the way down to bedrock?
A: Fred Flintstone.

■

Alex: "Do you know why I prefer pie to cake?"
Steve: "No, why?"
Alex: "Because pi can be squared."

■

Q: Why are Steve and Alex's puppies always being eaten in the Nether?
A: Because ghasts love hot dogs!

Q: What is Alex's favorite type of art?

A: Cubism.

Q: What happened to Alex when she first stepped into the Nether?
A: She was flabber-ghast-ed.

■

Q: What did Steve say to his girlfriend?
A: "I dig you."

■

Alex: "Did you hear that they are remodeling the floor at the daycare center?"
Steve: "Nope. What are they installing?"
Alex: "Infan-tiles!"

■

Q: How does Steve exercise?
A: He runs around the block.

■

Q: What happened when Alex spawned a Wither?
A: She didn't know *wither* to laugh or cry.

Q: How did Alex get Steve to stop texting her?
A: She blocked him.

■

Knock, knock.
Who's there?
Alex.
Alex, who?
Alex-plain later!

■

Q: What is Alex's favorite movie?
A: *How to Train Your Ender Dragon.*

■

Q: What did Alex say to the stupid zombie?
A: "I'd explain it to you, but your brain would explode."

■

Q: Why was Alex mad at the builder who told her to use a sturdier stone for her building?
A: She hates constructive criticism.

Alex: "If there were cars in Minecraft, what would the bumper stickers read?"
Steve: "I don't know. What?"
Alex: "Earth first. We'll mine other planets later."

■

Steve: "Why was the player thrilled when he found pumpkins instead of diamonds?"
Alex: "I don't know. Why?"
Steve: "Because in Minecraft, pumpkins are rarer than diamonds."

■

Steve: "How did the player hide from the creeper and the skeleton?"
Alex: "How?"
Steve: "He hid behind glass."

■

Steve: "What are a miner's three rules for finding gold?"
Alex: "I know. It's mine, mine, and mine."

Steve: "What did one PVP say to the other?"
Alex: "I don't know. What?"
Steve: "I won fair and square."

■

Steve: "Why would Picasso love Minecraft?"
Alex: "I don't know. Why?"
Steve: "Because he was a Cubist!"

■

Q: Why did Steve take a balloon ride in a thunderstorm?
A: He heard that every cloud has a silver lining.

■

Alex: "Did you know that *Annie* has a great Minecraft song?"
Steve: "No. What's it called?"
Alex: "It's a Hard-Block Life."

■

Q: What did one Steve say when he saw another Steve?
A: "Hi, Steve."

Q: What did Steve say to the other Steve when it was time to leave?
A: "Bye, Steve."

■

First player: "How does Steve chop down trees?"
Second player: "How *wood* I know?"

■

Q: Who is Steve's favorite action hero?
A: The Eggs-Terminator.

■

Q: What kind of music does Alex listen to?
A: Block and roll.

■

Q: Why did Steve have food poisoning?
A: He ate the rotting flesh from a zombie.

■

Alex: "How good is Minecraft?"
Steve: "It's top-Notch!"

Q: How does Steve pick his nose?
A: With a pickaxe.

■

Alex: "Hey, Steve, this game is too easy."
Steve: "Then step it up a Notch!"

■

Alex: "Hey, Steve, did you get the Minecraft jokes I sent you?"
Steve: "No, they're all blocked."

■

Q: What does Steve sleep on?
A: Bedrock.

■

Q: What did one Steve say to another Steve just before he killed him?
A: "Bye, Steve, bye!"

■

Q: Why is Steve so proud of his children?
A: Because they're chips off the old block.

Q: What did the Ender Dragon say when he saw Steve dressed in armor?

A: "Oh, no! Canned food."

■

Q: What did Steve say to another Steve?

A: "You're such a copycat!"

Q: How many Steves does it take to change a lightbulb?
A: None. There aren't any lightbulbs in Minecraft.

■

Q: Why did Steve cross the road?
A: To say hi to Steve.

■

Q: Why did Steve cross the road?
A: To get away from Steve.

■

Q: Why did the chicken cross the road?
A: Also to get away from Steve.

■

Q: Why couldn't Steve cross the road?
A: Because he hadn't built it yet.

■

Q: Why couldn't Steve get into the house?
A: The door was blocked.

Q: How many meals does Steve eat every day?
A: Three square.

■

Q: What did Steve say to the skeleton?
A: "I have a bone to pick with you."

■

Steve: "Did you hear about the new Minecraft movie?"
Alex: "Yes, it's a blockbuster!"

■

Alex: "You tell so many jokes!"
Steve: "It's true! And these jokes *Nether* end!"

■

Alex: "What is the national sport of Minecraft?"
Steve: "Boxing."

■

Alex: "Why couldn't the Minecraft player vote?"
Steve: "Because he was a miner."

Alex: "Why are there no carts in Minecraft?"
Steve: "Because square wheels don't roll well."

■

Alex: "Why are there no wagons in Minecraft?"
Steve: "Because square wheels don't roll well, either!"

■

Q: What's the difference between Alex and an archaeologist?
A: Alex hates finding skeletons underground.

Q: How did Steve make the player change directions?
A: He blocked her path.

■

Alex: "Why is your head shaped like a block?"
Steve: "Well, it's a long story. I was digging and came across a magic lamp. I rubbed it, and out popped a genie."
Alex: "What did you wish for?"
Steve: "See that beautiful mansion over there? I wished for that, and it appeared. Then I wished for the power to defeat the Ender Dragon. I think I messed up my third wish. I wished for a block head!"

■

First player: "Steve was so sad."
Second player: "How sad was he?"
First player: "He was so sad that he hit bedrock bottom."

■

Q: What has four legs and goes boom?
A: Two Alex's fighting over TNT.

Q: Why did Steve throw eggs at the creeper?
A: He wanted them ssscrambled.

■

Q: Why did Steve walk across the road?
A: Because there are no cars in Minecraft.

■

Q: What did the creeper say to Steve?
A: Sssurprise!

■

Q: What did the creeper say to Steve?
A: Nothing. It just blew up.

■

Q: What do you get when cross a spider with Alex?
A: Death.

■

Q: Why did Alex need homeowner's insurance?
A: Her house kept blowing up.

Q: Why does Steve like having a mooshroom as a roommate?
A: Because the mooshroom is a fungi.

■

Alex: "Why are there no cars in Minecraft?"
Steve: "Because I haven't invented the internal combustion engine yet."

■

Q: Why couldn't Steve finish writing his book?
A: He had writer's block.

■

Steve: "I'm writing this book for Minecraft players."
Alex: "Wow. Do you think people will get it?"
Steve: "Well, it's niche humor . . ."
Alex: "I would say it's *Notch* humor."

■

Steve: "Which came first, the chicken or the egg?"
Alex: "I don't know. Ask Notch."

■

Q: What did the TNT say to Steve?
A: "I'll blow you to pieces."

Q: What's Steve's favorite type of dancing?

A: Square dancing!

Steve: "How are amino acids related to Minecraft?"
Alex: "I don't know. How?"
Steve: "They're both building blocks of life."

■

Steve: "Why was the Minecraft player so good at boxing?"
Alex: "Why?"
Steve: "Because he could block a punch."

■

Q: What crime-catching skills do Minecraft police excel at?
A: Putting up road blocks.

■

Alex: "How many blocks fit in an empty chest?"
Steve: "One, because after one, it's no longer empty."

■

Q: Why doesn't Steve get invited to parties?
A: He's too square.

Q: Why does Steve have trouble solving problems?
A: He has trouble thinking outside the box.

■

Q: What is Steve's favorite party appetizer?
A: Cheese cubes.

■

Q: What does Alex do each time she slays a creeper?
A: Puts a Notch on her sword.

■

Q: Why couldn't Steve go on the Internet?
A: It was blocked.

■

Q: Why did Steve think Alex was hot?
A: She was on fire.

■

Q: Why did Alex think Steve was hot?
A: He was drowning in lava.

Q: What type of pizza does Alex like?
A: Sicilian.

■

Q: What did Steve say to his girlfriend?
A: "You stole 9.5 of my hearts!"

■

Q: What type of music can't Alex and Steve sing together?
A: A round.

■

Q: What type of floor did Alex put in the house she built for her pet snake?
A: Rep-tile.

■

Q: Why does Alex put spells on her armor?
A: It makes her an enchantress.

■

Steve: "What do you get when you cross a snake with a Minecraft builder?"
Alex: "A boa constructor."

Steve: "Why do Minecrafters build with blocks?"
Alex: "They can't build with spheres."

■

Q: Why did Steve wear rocks for shoes?
A: He thought they were cobbler-stones.

■

Q: What do you get when you cross a cave spider with Steve?
A: A dead Steve.

■

Q: What did Steve say to Alex?
A: "I dig your style."

■

Q: Why couldn't Alex answer Steve's question?
A: Her mind was blocked.

■

Alex: "What do you call a polar bear in Minecraft?"
Steve: "I don't know. What?"
Alex: "Lost, because there are no polar bears in Minecraft!"

Steve: “Can a player jump higher than a tree?”
Alex: “Of course, because trees can’t jump.”

■

Steve: “Knock, knock.”
Alex: “Who’s there?”
Steve: “Markus.”
Alex: “Markus who?”
Steve: “Markus down for two tickets to Minecon.”

■

Alex: “What’s stopping you from moving forward?”
Steve: “My mine’s blocked.”

■

Q: How did Alex know what move Steve was going to make?
A: She’s a *mine* reader.

■

Q: Why was Steve mad at Alex?
A; Because she took him for *granite*.

Alex: "How did the student learning Minecraft drown?"
Steve: "I don't know. How?"
Alex: "Her grades were below C-level."

■

Q: Why couldn't Steve stop reading a book about helium?
A: He was so fascinated that he couldn't put it down.

■

Q: What did Steve do with the dead iron golem?
A: Barium!

■

Q: Why didn't Alex want to hear the mountain joke?
A: Because she couldn't get over it. It was blocked.

■

Alex: "What did one square block say to the other square block?"
Steve: "I don't know. What?"
Alex: "You're pointless."

Q: Why did Steve have trouble finishing his term paper?
A: He had a mental block.

■

Alex: "How is Minecraft like soccer?"
Steve: "I don't know. How?"
Alex: "Both games last for hours, nobody scores, and millions of fans insist you just don't understand."

MINECRAFT LIMERICKS, POEMS AND HAIKUS

There once was a miner named Steve
Who was proud of all that he had achieved.
As he grew older,
His reflexes got bolder
And he decided never to leave!

■

Alex built a garden on Sunday
And caught a snake that was gray.
She tried her best to make him stay.
The snake, however, slithered away.

■

Alex constructed a zoo.
She always found something to do.
When it bored her, you know,
She walked to and fro,
Then reversed it and walked fro and to.

■

Alex likes to build.
Adding more colorful blocks,
Her world simply rocks.

■

Spawned in a new world.
Alex gathers resources.
First she collects wood.

■

A crafty good player named Steve
Would stop at nothing to deceive.
He played all night long,
Until his skills became strong,
And would stop at nothing, I believe.

■

Steve won't stop digging.
He searches in vain for jewels
And sparkling diamonds.

■

Oh no, here he goes.
Steve's falling down a tunnel.
Deeper, faster, SPLAT!

DID YOU KNOW...?

Did you know Steve originally had a goatee? It was shaved off because it looked like he was smiling all of the time!

Did you know that Alex caused controversy when she was first released partially because Mojang stated that Steve was a male and a female skin?

Did you know that there used to be a Steve, Beast Boy, Human, Rana, and Original Steve Mobs?

Did you know when Markus Persson, the creator of Minecraft, told his high school guidance counselor that he wanted to make video games, his counselor said that probably wouldn't happen?

CHAPTER 7

HEROBRINE

JOKES

Q: How does Herobrine spy on people?
A: He uses spyders.

■

Q: What did the pro Minecraft player say to Herobrine?
A: You sure ocelot of questions.

■

Q: What did Herobrine say to the ocelot?
A: Do what I tell you, ore else!

■

Q: How did Herobrine confuse a Minecraft fan?
A: He put him in a room full of empty boxes.

Q: What did Herobrine get when he pushed a music box down a mineshaft?

A: A-flat miner.

■

Q: Why was Herobrine sent to the doctor?

A: He had a virus.

Q: How did Herobrine slow down the computer?

A: He took a couple of bytes out of it.

■

Q: Why was Herobrine afraid to go to the delicatessen?

A: Because last time he went, the deli men tried to use him to make pickles.

■

Q: Why did Herobrine visit the seashore?

A: He wanted to visit Ocean Brine.

■

Q: What did Herobrine say when he looked into the mirror?

A: "Oh, no, my twin!"

■

Q: What did Herobrine do at lunchtime?

A: He took a byte out of your computer.

■

Q: Why did Herobrine keep sneezing?

A: He had a virus!

Q: How is Herobrine like a favorite Disney dog?

A: He makes your computer go goofy.

■

Q: Why was Herobrine in the computer?

A: Because he wanted a byte to eat.

■

Q: What's Herobrine's favorite snack?

A: Chips.

■

Q: How could you tell Herobrine was getting old?

A: He had memory loss.

Q: Did you hear the one about the bucket of salty water that saved the day?

A: Herobrine.

■

Q: Who isn't in any versions of Minecraft, yet players say they've spotted him?

A: Herobrine.

■

Q: What's another name for Herobrine?

A: A virus.

■

To err is human, and to blame it on Herobrine is even more so!

■

To err is human, but to really mess things up requires Herobrine!

MINECRAFT LIMERICKS, POEMS, AND HAIKUS

A legend by many he's called.
In the game of Minecraft he's installed.
His name is Herobrine.
He appears to live in the mine.
Oh no, now my screen has stalled.

■

The TNT exploded.
Actually, it imploded.
It missed Herobrine's face.
He wouldn't give up the chase.
I got him while I reloaded.

Deep into the game, Herobrine appears.
He's messing up the shaft mine gears.
I try my best to slay him.
Losing to him would be grim.
At last, I win and give three cheers.

■

As I stand on the ledge of a mine,
I create a potion to stop Herobrine.
He's causing my computer to glitch
And is making me twitch.
I vow to stop him right now.
If I only knew how.
I guess I will have to turn off the switch.

■

Is Herobrine a glitch?
He's definitely not a witch.
Some claim he's hidden inside the game.
Many others are here to proclaim.
That Notch created him as a hitch.

■

Is he a legend or is he real?
What is Herobrine's deal?
They say he's never been seen,
Though many say his shirt is green.
He looks just like Steve.
Others just don't believe.
They supposedly share the same type of skin.
Maybe they are just twins!

If you see two lights shining bright.
Beware, be quick, and take flight.
It's Herobrine coming after you.
You need a sword, one weapon or two.
You must slow him down with a brick.
On your feet, you must think quick.
TNT will do the trick!

Herobrine's a miner by trade.
You may spot him or he may fade.
He doesn't exist.
He's just a glitch.
Or your computer may need an upgrade.

■

An urban legend named Herobrine
Has a favorite pig he calls Heroswine.
He's not in the game's code.
Yet he can cause you to explode.
If you mistake him for Steve
Get out quickly and leave.

DID YOU KNOW...?

Did you know that Herobrine is said to be Notch's brother?

Did you know that Herobrine will attack any mob?

Did you know that Herobrine sometimes wears diamond armor?

Did you know that most players think Herobrine's a ghost?

Did you know that Herobrine cannot be killed?

MINECRAFT ADDICTS

You know you are addicted to Minecraft when you have fantasies of spotting Herobrine!

CHAPTER 8

WEAPONS, FLOWERS, AND JEWELS

JOKES

Q: Why did the sailor bring iron onto his ship?

A: He needed ores!

■

Q: Why don't miners mine in Oregon?

A: Because the ore is gone.

■

Q: What keeps a tree in place?

A: Square roots!

■

Q: What's red and invisible?

A: No roses!

Q: How do you prevent creepers from digging in your garden?

A: Hide their shovels.

■

Q: Why does the player prefer silver over gold?

A: Because she digs silver and pans gold.

Sticks and stones may break my bones, but now I can build a pickaxe!

■

Q: Why did Markus Persson create Minecraft?
A: He thought it would be ore-some.

■

Q: Did you hear the joke about the broken sword?
A: It's pointless.

■

Q: If a tree falls in a forest and there's nobody to see it fall, does it hit the ground?
A: The tree floats until you chop it down with an axe.

■

Q: Where do miners like to relax?
A: In a rocking chair.

■

Q: Where else do miners like to relax?
A: On bedrock.

Q: What did the player say while he continued to break rocks?

A: "Rock on!"

■

Q: What did the Minecraft pro tell the noob?

A: "May the quartz be with you."

■

Q: Why did the miner cry when his friend left?

A: He was very sedimental.

■

Q: What is The King's favorite sing-a-long song?

A: "If I Had a Hammer."

■

Q: Why did the player cross the lava?

A: Because there were twenty-nine diamonds on the other side.

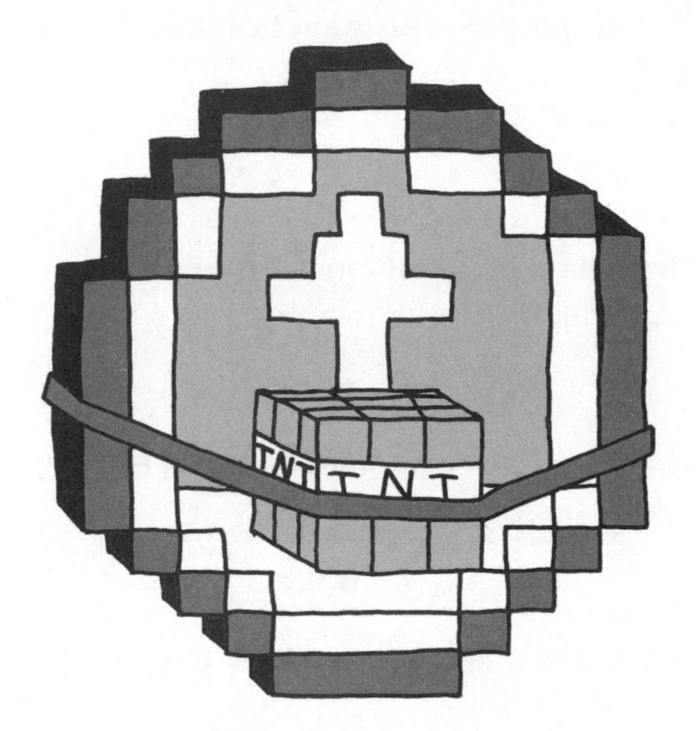

Q: What do you get if you cross a redstone clock with TNT?

A: A ticking time bomb.

■

Q: Why is a noob like an uncut diamond?

A: Both are rough around the edges and shine with some polish.

MINECRAFT LIMERICKS, POEMS, AND HAIKUS

A very smart player named Rob,
Tried to hide from a mob
By building two-block-tall flowers
That gave him hidden powers.
Oh, Rob, what a good job!

■

There was a young miner named Robby.
He developed a terrible hobby.
He'd knock on your door,
Drop his pickaxe on the floor,
And use TNT to blow up your new lobby.

■

In real life we pick them,
Removing roots and entire stem.
We don't want them in our gardens.
Yet in Minecraft we grant them pardons.
Because we know dandelions are pretty gems.

■

Flowers generate on dirt and grass blocks.
Dandelions and poppies grow around the rocks.
Even in biomes covered in snow,
Roses and tulips continue to grow.

■

Who ever heard of flowers blooming in snow?
We know in Minecraft it is possible though.
In a snowstorm, poppies add beautiful hues.
Despite the snow, the landscape continues to amuse.
These hardy flowers battle all elements to grow.
In the end they triumph with a decorative show.

■

There once was a player named Joel.
He mined in the dark, don't you know.
He needed light
To make things bright.
Now, Joel uses sticks and coal.

■

There once was a Minecraft player named Moe.
He searched for diamonds high and low.
They're the hardest, strongest, and rarest to find.
Despite this, he didn't mind.
Soon he saw their brilliant glow.

■

There was a young player named Max.
He wielded a giant pickaxe.
He killed a large mob
And loved doing his job
And piled them up in big stacks.

■

Chopping down a tree.
I am incredibly strong.
Using my bare hands.

■

Digging block by block,
I suddenly hit bedrock.
Searching for diamonds
And searching for gold.
Playing Minecraft never gets old.

■

With arrow in hand I take aim.
I simply love playing this game.
Watching things explode—
Buildings fall and erode.
Nothing about Minecraft is lame!

■

Roses are square.
Dandelions are square.
Tulips are square.
What do you expect?
This is Minecraft—everything is square!

■

There was an old witch.
She dug in a ditch
And found diamonds that glowed
Not too far under the road.
Now this witch is very rich!

■

Diamonds underground
Lying there just underfoot.
Beware: hot lava.

■

With a big pickaxe
I spend too much time digging
TNT's faster!

DID YOU KNOW...?

Did you know that the main flowers at Jeb's wedding were peonies?

Did you know that a Minecraft ice farm can also be used as an ordinary skating rink?

Did you know that diamond swords do the most damage?

Did you know that the wood sword does the least damage?

Did you know that in Minecraft flowers grow underground?

Did you know that not all compasses point north? In Minecraft, a compass points to the last bed you slept in!

Did you know that if you sleep in a bed, you'll skip to the next morning?

Did you know that emeralds, diamonds, gold, and redstone can only be mined with an iron pickaxe?

Did you know that emeralds can only be found in the extreme hills biome?

Did you know that the three weapons in Minecraft are lava, swords, and bows?

Did you know that swords can be made out of wood, stone, iron, gold, and diamonds?

Did you know that there are five kinds of armor in Minecraft? They are leather, gold, iron, chain, and diamonds.

Did you know that you can only get chain armor in creative mode or from a villager trade?

Did you know that roses are rarer than dandelions?

Did you know that silverfish hide in rocks and stone?

Did you know that the Ender Dragon will pass right through obsidian, end stone, and bedrock without destroying them?

Did you know that "Mojang," the name of the Swedish video game company founded by Markus Persson, is a Swedish word meaning "gadget"?

MINECRAFT ADDICTS

You know you are addicted to Minecraft when you try to plant flowers in the snow!

CHAPTER 9

ORESPAWN, MUTANT CREATURES, AND TWILIGHT FOREST MODS

JOKES

Q: What do you get when you cross Mobzilla with The King?

A: Total destruction.

■

Q: What did Mobzilla give to The King?

A: A royal pain.

■

Q: Why was the hydra put in charge?

A: Because he provides hydra-electric power.

Creeper: "How many weapons are there in the Orespawn mod?"
Zombie: "Who cares? All it takes is just one hit and you will explode."

■

Q: What's the best way to talk to a mutant creature?
A: From a distance!

Q: How do mutant zombies like their meals?
A: Runny.

■

Q: Where is a mutant creeper's favorite place to visit?
A: Lake Eerie.

■

Q: How can you tell a good mutant creeper from a bad one?
A: If he's a good mutant creeper, you will be able to talk about it later.

■

Q: Who did the mutant zombie call when he lost his head?
A: A head hunter.

■

Q: How did the mutant zombie clear his throat?
A: He spent all day gargoyling.

■

Q: On which days do mutant zombies eat?
A: Chewsday.

Q: What do single mutant zombies do at parties?

A: They go around looking for edible bachelors.

■

Q: What do you call a polite, friendly, and good-looking mutant creature?

A: A failure!

■

Q: Why do mutant creature mobs like bell-bottom pants?

A: Because they are mod!

Q: Why did the mutant zombie take his nose off?
A: He wanted to see how it runs!

■

Q: What should you do if a mutant creeper crashes through your front door?
A: Crash through your back door!

■

Q: What did the mommy mutant zombie say to her children?
A: "It's not polite to talk with someone in your mouth!"

■

First Mutant Zombie: "See that player over there?"
Second Mutant Zombie: "Yes."
First Mutant Zombie: "Well, she just rolled her eyes at me."
Second Mutant Zombie: "You should roll them back to her. She might need them!"

■

Q: What do they serve for lunch at mutant zombie school?
A: Human beans, boiled legs, pickled bunions, and eyes cream.

First Mutant Zombie: "Am I late for dinner?"
Second Mutant Zombie: "Yes, everyone's already been eaten."

■

Q: Why should you duck if a hydra sneezes?
A: He has fire breath.

Q: What did the mutant zombie vacationing on a cruise say to the ship's server at dinner time?
A: "Hold the menu, and bring me the passenger list."

■

Q: What did the blown-up mutant creeper's headstone read?
A: "Here he lies in pieces."

Q: What did the mutant creeper say to the mutant Enderman?
A: "Stop sucking me in!"

■

Q: What's scarier than a normal Enderman?
A: A mutant Enderman.

■

Q: How is the hydra's fireball attack like TNT?
A: It takes a few seconds before exploding when it hits the ground.

■

Q: Why does everyone like the Twilight Forest mod?
A: Because their habitat is filled with giant mushrooms and everyone knows mushrooms are fungis!

■

Q: What does the Nether and Twilight Forest realm have in common?
A: They both have glowstones that grow there naturally.

■

Q: Who has the voice of Death?
A: The mutant Enderman.

Q: Why were the players so hungry?

A: They were attacked by mosquito swarms.

■

Q: Why are mosquito swarms so annoying to players?

A: Because they get under their skin.

Q: What's a mutant creature mod's favorite form of art?
A: Modernism.

■

Q: Why are mosquito swarms so annoying to players?
A: Because they get under their skin.

■

Knock, knock.
Who's there?
Anna.
Anna, who?
Anna another swarm of mosquitoes.

■

Knock, knock.
Who's there?
Raven.
Raven who?
Raven lunatic player if you don't open this door!

MINECRAFT LIMERICKS, POEMS, AND HAIKUS

Exploring Twilight Forest mod is enthralling.
Perhaps it's the light from glowstones sprawling?
Discovering new creatures like rams, deer, and fireflies,
Makes this realm one that I prize
And adds a new level to my calling.

■

There once was a large Minotaur.
He's prepared to start a war.
Stay out of his line of vision,
For if he sees you, it will be his decision
To charge at you like a wild boar.

■

There once was a mutant Enderman named Bob.
He acted like such a terrible slob.
He never stayed clean
And was so terribly mean
That he angered numerous mobs!

■

DID YOU KNOW...?

Did you know that the Orespawn mod added more than 15 weapons, 100 bosses, and 60 mobs?

Did you know that if The King battled Mobzilla that there would be nothing left?

Did you know that the Orespawn mod has a ton of weapons and tools?

Did you know the Orespawn mod also has armor, mobs, and bosses?

Did you know that a mutant Enderman can carry four blocks and can also throw them at you?

Did you know that time travel slows the hydra down so it's easier to escape from him?

Did you know that mosquito swarms don't fly?

Did you know that mosquito swarms make loud buzzing sounds when you are near?

Did you know that deer living in the Overworld make the same sounds as cows?

CHAPTER 10

MINECRAFT PLAYERS

JOKES

First player: "Hey, what are you reading?"
Second player: "A review of a new Minecraft YouTube video."
First player: "What does it say?"
Second player: "It's iron-y, comedy gold, *glassic*, and will have you lava-ing in your face."

■

Q: What are Minecraft YouTubers called?
A: Blockheads!

■

Q: Why did the video game player cross the road?
A: To play Minecraft!

Q: What does a proud Minecraft dad call his son?
A: A chip off the old block.

■

First player: "Why is a fire drill not a good idea in Minecraft?"
Second player: "Why?"
First player: "Because in school we line up and act orderly. In Minecraft, when there's a fire, you need to run!"

■

Q: What do you call it when your dad beats you at Minecraft?
A: Mid-life crisis.

■

Mom of Minecraft player: "I wish there was a game on US history that's as popular as Minecraft."
Dad of Minecraft player: "Why?"
Mom of Minecraft player: "Because our son flunked his history test and he knows everything there is and more about Minecraft."

Q: What's a Minecraft player's favorite food?
A: *Notch-os*!

■

Q: Why can't Minecraft players get anything done?
A: Because they never get a round to it!

MINECRAFT LIMERICKS, POEMS, AND HAIKUS

There once was a player named Ray.
He sat down at his computer and started to play.
He clicked on Minecraft
And almost fell into a mineshaft.
And decided to play all day!

■

There once was a player named Mary.
Of hostile mobs she grew wary.
A fierce battle she won,
Defeating them was pure fun,
Even though it was quite hairy.

■

There once was a player, a kind fellow,
Who dyed sheep a very bright yellow.
Red, blue, and bright green,
All had a perfect sheen.
This fellow was also quite mellow.

■

An old ghast respawned from the past,
Entered the player's room with a blast.
He broke all the blocks,
Turning everything into tiny rocks.
He is such a pain in the gasp!

■

There once was a player named Dave.
He was known to give sheep a close shave.
He fought creepers and ghasts,
Exploding them with blasts.
Everyone said that Dave was quite brave.

DID YOU KNOW...?

Did you know that Minecraft is the most popular video game and has sold more than 42 million units?

Did you know that Minecraft has updates every single day?

Did you know that fans create new videos on YouTube about Minecraft every day?

Did you know that the only weapons skeletons use are bows and arrows?

MINECRAFT ADDICTS

You know you're addicted to Minecraft when you see a newborn baby and say, "Oh, what a cute noob!"

You know you're addicted to Minecraft when you try to get your teacher to let you do your book report on Minecraft!

You know you're addicted to Minecraft when the only time you see your parents is when you come down for dinner.

You know you're addicted to Minecraft when you put "Mastered Minecraft" on your resume.

You know you're addicted to Minecraft when you ask your doctor how many lives you have left.

You know you're addicted to Minecraft when you refuse to go outside because of the poor sound quality and shoddy graphics.

You know you're addicted to Minecraft when you name your kids Steve and Alex!

You know you're addicted to Minecraft when you get angry that real sand doesn't float.

You know you're addicted to Minecraft when you start saving up for a real diamond pickaxe.

You know you are addicted to Minecraft when you go to rock shops looking to buy redstone!

You know you're addicted to Minecraft when your mom is going on and on about something and you try to pause her.

You know you're addicted to Minecraft when you can't understand why your real wooden pickaxe won't break solid stone.

You know you're addicted to Minecraft when you think you can just gather lava and carry it back to your forge!

You know you are addicted to Minecraft when you dream in pixels!

You know you're addicted to Minecraft when you wish every day is update day!

You know you're addicted to Minecraft when you do a quick scan of every room you enter, looking for creepers.

You know you're addicted to Minecraft when someone asks you your age and you reply, "Level 14!"

You know you're addicted to Minecraft when someone asks you to tell them about the meaning of life and you say you have no idea when that version is coming out.

You know you're addicted to Minecraft when you miss two days of school and think, *that was a short game!*

You know you're addicted to Minecraft when you go outside and the sun hurts your eyes.

You know you're addicted to Minecraft when you think your fingers are in the best shape ever!

You know you're addicted to Minecraft when someone yells "Fire!" and you look for the blazes.

You know you're addicted to Minecraft when you dig a hole in your backyard looking for diamonds.

You know you're addicted to Minecraft when you don't turn off your lights at night because you think spiders will spawn!

You know you're addicted to Minecraft when you see something in the corner of your eye that's green!

You know you're addicted to Minecraft when you only eat cube-shaped foods.

You know you're addicted to Minecraft when you add an extra "s" to words with "s" in them.

You know you're addicted to Minecraft when the tea kettle whistles and you think you have a creeper in your house.

You know you're addicted to Minecraft if you think you need to drink a bucket of milk if you get bit by a spider.

You know you're addicted to Minecraft when you have nightmares about creepers and ghasts.

You know you're addicted to Minecraft if you think your cat is an ocelot and your dog is a wolf.

You know you're addicted to Minecraft when someone hisses at you and you yell, "Creeper!"

You know you're addicted to Minecraft when you draw squares instead of circles in your art class.

You know you're addicted to Minecraft when you punch a door and expect it to open.

You know you're addicted to Minecraft when you put "Builder" on your resume.

You know you've been playing Minecraft too long when you try to use sugar cubes to build your living room furniture!

You know you're addicted to Minecraft when you start each conversation talking about Minecraft.

You know you're addicted to Minecraft when you draw a square sun in art class.

You know you're addicted to Minecraft when it's no longer just a game for you!

You know you're addicted to Minecraft when you compare the real world to Minecraft at least once a day.

You know you're addicted to Minecraft when you write lists of all the mobs and mods!

UPROARIOUS Riddles FOR MINECRAFTERS

CHAPTER 1

WHAT AM I?

I like to swim, I like to fly
I like to walk, I love to try . . .
But you only see me when I die.
What am I?
Fish.

■

I'm red, blue, anything you want me to
I reach the sky, quite so high.
What am I?
Fireworks.

■

As brittle as the sand, but hard as rock
I'll take you to a new place, and then back.
What am I?
Obsidian.

You can eat me, and I'm orange, but in *Minecraft,* there are no oranges.
What am I?
A carrot.

■

You built me but I will destroy you.
What am I?
TNT.

■

I'm like a daisy
And I'm always wavy
I'm a special kind of flower
That has a fair amount of power.
What am I?
Poppy.

■

Send me away
But I will come back
Use me the right away
I'll provide a nice snack.
What am I?
Fishing rod.

Amidst the chaos, there I stand
Never warm, yes I am cold
Come to me, full of life
And thus begins your time of strife.
What am I?
The End.

■

I can be black or white
I'm small, and I don't bite
I'm soft, I walk . . . if I'm all right.
What am I?
Sheep.

Grumble, grumble
I always mumble.
What am I?
A ghast.

■

Hot like fire, float like a breeze?
I come from a mob
A fiery blob.
What am I?
A ghast fireball.

■

I'm sad but not blue
I'm friendly but not to you
Sorry for what I'm about to do—
BANG!
What am I?
A creeper.

■

I like to hide, I like to swim
I'll get close to you, if that's my whim!
What am I?
Silverfish.

I can hold a ton of treasures, more than you ever would think possible. Don't leave me unattended—I'll go fast!
What am I?
A Chest.

■

I am as numerous as the stars,
I can be used to tell time
Or create a sculpture.
What am I?
Sand.

■

I don't like Creepers
So I'll get them from standing away many meters.
What am I?
Bows and arrows.

■

I shine but not so bright
My brethren shines brighter.
What am I?
A redstone torch.

I beep, I bop, I thud, I thwop.
What am I?
A Note Block.

■

I am devastatingly destructive, and yet I am unarmed. What am I?
A Creeper.

■

I fly through the sky and maybe right through you. But I am not a ghost. What am I?
A Ghast.

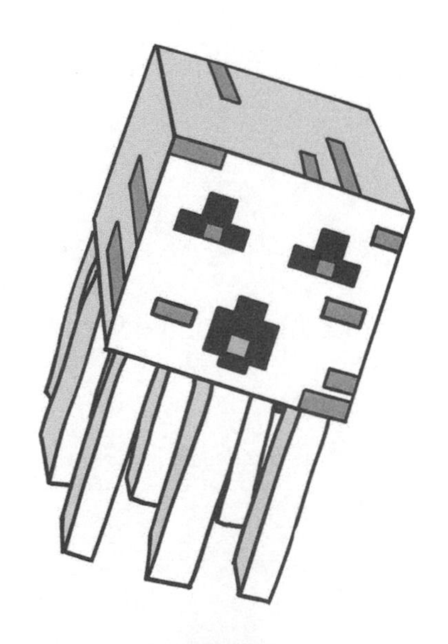

I live though I am dead. What am I?
A Zombie.

■

Don't get all hot and bothered trying to figure out what I am!
A Blaze.

■

When you're with me, you stop on green and go on red. What am I?
A Watermelon!

■

I'm a *Minecraft* thing that's full of ticks . . . but I'm not a Dog or a Wolf. What am I?
A Clock.

■

I don't have any "armies" but I can destroy you just the same. What am I?
A Creeper.

I am but one, but I wear many hats. What am I?
A Wither.

■

I have many rings but no fingers. What am I?
A Tree.

■

Open your eyes and you will not see me.
Close your eyes and you will. What am I?
Darkness.

■

I rattle, but a baby wouldn't like me. What am I?
A Skeleton.

■

I'll make you hungry while grossing you out at the same time. What am I?
A Husk.

I like to attack, but if I'm not attacking, you're attacking me, and then I'm running away from the attack. What am I?
An Evoker.

■

I am evoked, but I am not an Evoker. What am I?
A Vex.

■

I can stand in the sun all day, but my skin doesn't burn. What am I?
A Husk.

■

I can give you the power to walk through walls. What am I?
A door.

■

I'm orange on top and white on the bottom. What am I?
A Snow Golem.

I'll offer you a tip, but you should always turn it down—and quickly. What am I?

A Stray (with a slowness-inflicting arrow).

■

I make a noise once . . . but you'll hear me over and over again. What am I?

A stray (stray . . . stray . . . stray . . .).

■

I am like a Torch, but I am not a Torch Block. What am I?

A Jack-O-Lantern.

I have six sides, but I am but one thing. What am I?
A Block!

■

I am a Hostile, except when I'm a building Block. What am I?
Slime.

■

I am the only Ore that can't be mined with a tool made out of myself. What am I?
Gold ore.

■

If you can't see in the sea, I can help you see in the sea, if you can see enough in the sea to see me. What am I?
A Sea Lantern.

■

I am a Block, but you can't hold me, place me, or mine me, or see me. What am I?
An air block.

I have lots of eyes but cannot see. What am I?
A potato.

■

I am a rock, but am softer than dirt. What am I?
Netherrack.

■

I'm a crop and provide energy, and you may think I could help you walk, but I can't. What am I?
Sugar cane.

■

I fly high in the nether, and the Ender dragon is my mortal enemy. What am I?
Wither.

■

When you see a potion, trouble is brewing. What am I?
A witch.

■

I come in a Hostile Mob of three . . . but I am not a trio of witches. What am I?
Wither.

I'm wet, but I'm not a River or an Ocean. I am land but I am not the Desert or the Forest. What am I?
Swampland.

■

If you want to come to this biome, you'll just have to go with the flow. What am I?
River.

■

Wooden you like to know which biome I am?
Forest.

■

My name means ordinary but I'm anything but. What am I?
Plains.

■

I am high, but not mountain high. What am I?
Extreme Hills.

If you want to visit me, dry, dry again. What am I?
Desert.

■

A newfound wave of excitement will wash over you when visiting me. What am I?
Ocean.

■

I'm up above you and all around, but I'm also where the story goes no further. What am I?
The End.

■

I am a block but I am not
You can see me, but you cannot
I exist, that much is true
Air Block.

■

I am blue, with a heart of gold
I am new, still I look old
Deep in the water, so you're told
Ocean Monument.

Am I really that disgusting?
I only want a part of you
I have no use for all of you
. . . or I'll just find somebody new
Zombie.

■

A visit here is like a day at the, well, you know. What am I?
Beach.

■

Don't bungle this or you'll die on the vine.
Jungle.

CHAPTER 2

A MOB OF HOSTILE MOB JOKES

How do Guardians stay healthy?
Plenty of Vitamin Sea.

■

Why do Withers look so tough?
Because they wear Wither jackets.

■

What's a Shulk's favorite superhero?
The Incredible Shulk!

■

Why did the Skeleton shoot his arrows?
Because he's heartless.

A fiery Hostile attacked a Cow in the plains every day for a few weeks.
It was an amazingly crazy Blaze graze phase!

■

Skeletons have a hard time making friends.
They're such lonely boneys.

■

Slime think everybody loves them. Whenever they come up it's always "ooze" and "aggggghhhhhhs!"

■

What makes the Guardian special among Hostiles?
It's very so-fish-ticated.

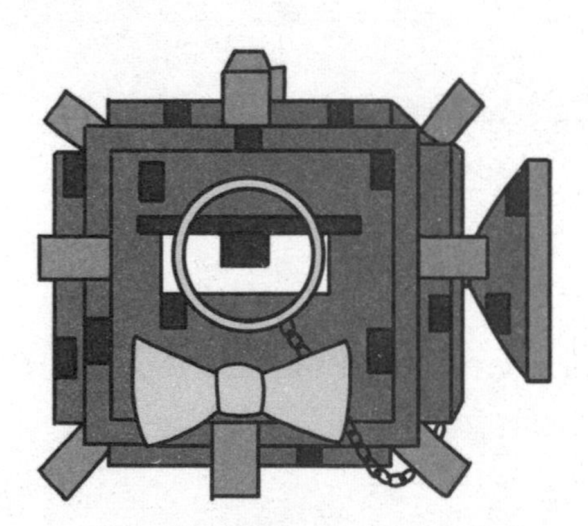

What time do you see Zombies in *Minecraft*?
At ate o'clock.

■

Why did the Zombie eat the Skeleton?
He wanted his bone and marrow.

■

How can you always beat a Zombie?
If you're the kind of person who has to get the last sword in.

■

Why wasn't the Vex much of an opponent?
It was flew season.

■

What floats and hisses?
A Ghast that learned how to speak Creeper.

■

Why don't Skeletons like the summer?
They're afraid of sunburns.

Why did the Ghast invade a tower?
It was in high spirits.

■

What's the most dangerous job in *Minecraft*?
Being an Evoker's dentist.

■

Can you name 30 creatures from *Minecraft*?
29 Creepers and a Ghast.

■

What's the heaviest mob in *Minecraft*?
Skele-tons.

■

What day are Zombies most likely to attack?
Chewsday.

■

What do Shulkers like on their pizza?
Purpuroni.

What do you call the first player who discovered a Blaze?
Toast!

■

Why do the Witches wear black hats?
To keep their heads warm.

■

Where do Zombie Pigmen buy their weapons?
Hamazon!

■

What kind of tests do Vexes take?
Vexaminations.

■

How do Vexes learn to fly?
They just wing it.

■

What's the difference between a fly and a Vex?
A Vex can fly, but a fly can't Vex.

Why couldn't the Zombie Pigman get out of lava?
Because he was a slow-pork.

How do Skeletons remain so calm when they're attacking?
Because nothing gets under their skin!

Will Shulkers always blend into their purpur shells to hide?
Yep, you can be Shulk they will!

■

What do a Blaze and a light source have in common?
One will scorch and the other is a Torch.

■

How did the Spider find a Spider Jockey?
It asked its hairy godmother.

■

How do you stop a Zombie Pigman?
Put him in hamcuffs.

■

How do Guardians fight off invaders?
Very e-fish-iently.

■

How does a Shulker talk to other Shulkers?
With a shell phone.

What happened when the Magma Cube wandered into an icy biome?
There was a lava-lanche!

■

Why did the Magma Cube attack?
It's just his way of saying, "I lava you."

■

Where do Magma Cubes go to the bathroom?
The lava-tory.

■

What do Magma Cubes eat?
Anything with lots of f-lava.

■

Why are Creepers so angry?
You would be too if you had green skin, no arms, and could explode at a moment's notice.

What do you get when you cross a Shulker with a Guardian?
A Hostile that is very shell-fish.

■

How do Shulkers know when the player is approaching?
They use a shelloscope.

■

Where's the best place to learn about Witches?
Witchapedia.

■

Where's the best place to learn about how Hostile cubes work?
In a Magmazine.

■

What did the overworked Evoker do?
It decided to lay low for a while.

■

What did the Skeleton say when he ran out of arrows?
"Shoot."

When something in *Minecraft* seems fishy . . . it's probably a Guardian.

■

Did you hear about Steve getting the Evoker with a sword?
It was his trusty Evoker Poker.

■

Did you hear about the Hostile who snuck onto Steve's boat?
It was a Ghast by the mast.

■

How do Guardians keep their breath fresh?
With monu-mints.

■

Why are Withers so good at baseball?
They always turn out a triple play.

■

Why are Ghasts white?
Because they got so afraid when they saw another Ghast!

What is a Vex's dream car?
A Vexus.

■

What do a fang-armed Hostile and Chickens have in common?
One's an Evoker, and one's a yolker.

■

What's an Evoker's favorite holiday?
Fangs-giving.

■

What kind of parties do Evokers like best?
Teeth parties.

■

How do Evokers stay healthy?
Bite-amins.

■

Where do you find a Skeleton?
Just follow the arrows.

When are you most likely to run into Skeletons?
During the graveyard shift.

■

What do you call it when a Skeleton drops something valuable?
A bone-us!

■

Why should you stay away from a Vex?
Because smoking is bad for you!

■

Where do Desert Zombies shop for their clothes?
In the Husk-y section.

■

What are rotten but not forgotten?
Husks.

■

Why did the Desert Zombies stalk Steve?
Husk because!

Why did the Husk go to the desert?
Because it heard it was the hot place to be!

■

What will a Vex attack?
What have you got?

■

How do you get a Vindicator to attack?
Just axe!

■

What do you call a stray?
Chilled to the bone!

■

When's the one time you'll always run into an Evoker?
Tooth-hurty.

■

What did the Evoker say after it bit Steve?
"Fangs!"

What do you call a Desert Zombie's odor?
A Husk musk.

Why do Husks sound so raspy?
They eat a lot of rasp-berries.

What's the difference between *Minecraft* and an Evoker?
One has bytes and the other has bites.

■

What did Steve say to the Vindicator when he needed emeralds?
"Can't we just drop this?"

■

Where do Vexes live?
Vexico.

■

What goes *clang bang*?
A Creeper holding a bell.

■

What do you get when you cross an Evoker and a Skeleton?
A Hostile that bites your knees.

■

Why didn't the Evoker eat a big meal?
He just wanted a few bites.

What do you call a Guardian with no eye?
A Guardan.

■

What's the difference between a Guardian and an Ocelot?
One drops fish . . . and the other never would!

■

What do you call it when a Guardian squeaks so loud that it summons another Guardian?
A squeakuel.

■

How can you have stairs underwater?
When it's a Guardian and they're stares.

■

What's the difference between an especially fiery hostile and a Guardian?
One is a Blazer, and the other has a laser.

What should you never make with a Guardian?
Eye contact!

■

What kind of structures could Guardians build with?
Laser beams!

■

Where do Shulkers power up?
At the Shell Station.

■

What's a Shulker's favorite old album?
Purpur Rain.

■

What's a Shulker's favorite game?
Hide-and-Hide.

■

What's a Shulker's favorite kitchen gadget?
A blender.

Why is the Guardian such an effective Hostile?
Because of its laser-like focus!

■

Why was the Skeleton after the miner?
He had a bone to pick.

■

Where do Evokers and Vindicators live?
In a nice Illage.

■

What did Steve say when he grabbed some dropped Emeralds?
“Finally, I’ve been Vindicator-ated!”

■

Why didn’t the Guardian attack?
Out of sight, out of mind.

■

What does a Ghast do on the Internet?
It tweets.

What do you get if you cross a monkey and a Creeper?
A baboom!

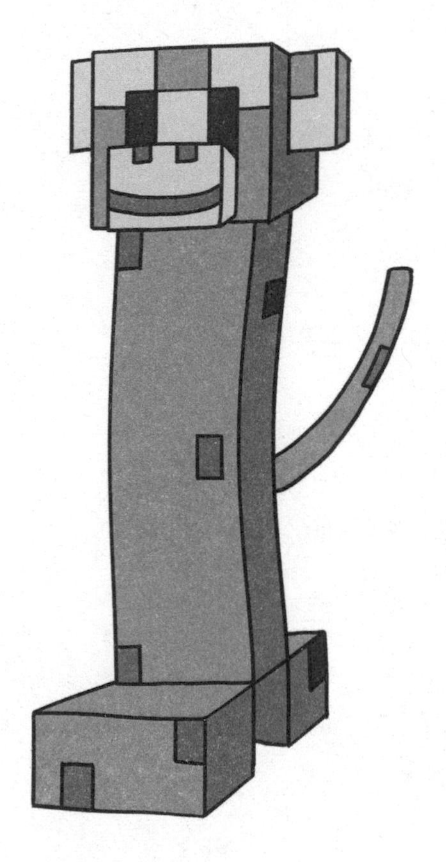

What's more annoying than a Skeleton shooting bows and arrows at you?
Ten Skeletons shooting bows and arrows at you.

Why did the Creeper never get called on in school?
Because it never raised its hand.

■

Why can't you trust a Zombie Pigman?
They always squeal.

■

Why do Witches like football?
For all the huts.

■

Who's a Zombie Pigman's favorite artist?
Pig-casso

■

What's white, floaty, and wears sunglasses?
A Ghast on vacation.

■

Where do Blazes eat?
At Sizzler.

CHAPTER 3

FOOD, FARMS, AND FARMERS

What do Creepers eat for breakfast?
Sssssscrambled eggs.

■

How do Creepers get in their vegetables each day?
With a big sssssalad.

■

What drink should be avoided at all costs in *Minecraft*?
"Tea and tea."

■

Why did the Farmer plant blocks of Hay?
He wanted straw berries.

What's the most dangerous Easter candy in *Minecraft*?
Marshmallow Creeps.

■

The creator of *Minecraft* eats this for lunch.
Notch-os.

■

What do Miners eat at the movies?
Gemmy Bears.

■

What did Steve say after he ate a sheep?
"I can't believe I ate the wool thing!"

■

How do Minecrafters start their day?
With a cup of Builders' tea.

■

What do Minecrafters eat at 4 p.m.?
Tea and stones.

What do Minecrafters put in their tea?
Sugar cubes.

What kind of cookies does Steve eat?
Ore-e-os.

How are plants in *Minecraft* like math?
The square roots.

■

What kind of food might you find atop a wall?
A wall-nut.

■

What do they serve in the Ice Plains Biome?
Chili!

■

What do Creepers eat for breakfast?
Rice Creepies.

■

What do you call a smiling Pumpkin?
A pumpgrin!

■

How do Ghasts make sandwiches?
With fresh dread.

What kind of milk do you get from a pampered cow?
Spoiled milk.

■

What do you get from a Cow in the Tundra Biome?
Ice cream.

■

How can you tell if a Minecrafter has been eating your sandwich?
There are "8 bits" taken out of it.

■

What do Spiders in abandoned mineshafts eat?
Corn on the cobwebs.

■

What are all meals in *Minecraft*?
Square meals.

■

What do you feed trees in *Minecraft?*
Knuckle sandwiches.

Where does a Minecrafter eat cookies?
Mrs. Fields.

■

Where does a Minecrafter buy chocolate?
Rocky Mountain Chocolate Company.

■

Where does Steve eat burgers?
Steve-in-the-Box.

■

Where does Steve get burgers and shakes?
Shake Shack.

■

What cool rock n' roll restaurant do Minecrafters like?
The Hard Rock Café.

■

What's red and cold?
An apple in a cold biome.

What ice cream do Minecrafters eat?
Rocky Road.

What do *Minecraft* ore eat?
Pom-a-granites.

■

What's a Minecrafter's favorite cereal?
Cocoa Pebbles.

What's a Minecrafter's favorite candy?
Rock candy.

■

How does Steve like his soda?
On the rocks!

■

What fruit prevents Steve from catching a cold?
Ore-anges.

■

What kind of fish do Minecrafters like best?
Walleye.

■

How did Notch fix a glitch in the farming elements of the game?
With a cabbage patch.

■

What's a Minecrafter's favorite baked dessert?
Cobbler.

What kind of salad is served in the colder biomes?
Ice-berg lettuce.

■

How do Minecrafters take their pizza?
Plain.

■

What do you feed an Enderman?
Evaporated milk.

■

What's a Minecrafter's favorite kind of cheese?
Swiss, because it's full of holes.

■

What's a Minecrafter's *other* favorite kind of cheese?
Cottage cheese.

■

Why didn't the Minecrafter have to pay for dinner?
It was on the house!

What do you feed a Sword?
Slice cream.

■

What will spawn if you plant seeds at night?
Moonbeams.

■

Where do crops hang out before they sprout?
The Wheating room.

■

What do Farmers eat for breakfast?
Wheaties.

■

What *Minecraft* room can you not enter?
A mushroom.

■

What did the Fishing pole say to the Fish?
"Catch you later!"

What is green and jumps?
A Watermelon with hiccups!

■

What's brown and has wheels?
Wheat. (We were kidding about the wheels.)

■

What do Minecrafters order at a Mexican restaurant?
An ore-ito.

■

Did you hear about the carrots that were about to fall off Steve's workbench?
They were some edgy veggies.

■

What did Steve take to eat during a mining day?
A boxed lunch.

■

What do Minecrafters collect?
Lunchboxes.

What side dish do Minecrafters love?
Coal slaw.

■

Where do Minecrafters go to have buffet?
Golden Corral.

■

Why didn't the Minecrafter like dropped meat?
It was a little too raw for him.

■

What do Minecrafters eat for lunch?
Minekraft Macaroni and Cheese.

■

What did the glowstone eat for lunch?
Just a light meal.

■

How do Minecrafters keep their breath fresh?
With develop-mints.

Where do Rabbits go to eat?
IHOP.

How do you make lemons in *Minecraft*?
Rearrange the "Melons."

Why couldn't the Minecrafter make any more sugar cane?
She was out of stalk.

■

What crop do you never have a little of?
Cocoa—because you wind up with a choco-lot of it.

■

What potato chips do Minecrafters eat?
Roofles.

■

Why did the Minecrafter plant potatoes and carrots?
He wanted to get back to his roots.

■

What did Alex say when Steve brought her fresh sugar cane?
"That's sweet!"

■

What drink will you find underground in *Minecraft*?
Coal-a.

How long does it take crops to grow in Farmland?
About a wheat.

■

Why did the player hide his chest in Farmland?
He was playing Crops and Robbers.

■

What crop is the most fun to grow?
Wheeeeeeeat!

■

What happened when cocoa got planted near an Ender Dragon?
Cocoa Puffs!

■

What's brown, round, and found underground?
Potatoes.

■

Which mushrooms should you use in *Minecraft*?
We don't know, it's soup to you!

What do Minecrafters eat for breakfast?
Dragon eggs and Beacon.

■

What happened when Steve ate too many pickles?
He turned into Herobrine.

■

What kind of chocolates do Minecrafters prefer?
Bomb-bombs.

■

What's another way to get gold in *Minecraft*?
Find 24 carrots!

■

Why was the farm upset?
It was just irrigated.

■

Where would you find corn in *Minecraft*?
In a Cobweb block.

This room can only be brown or red. What kind of room is it?
A mushroom.

■

In what video game can you grow pickles?
Brinecraft.

■

What do Minecrafters order at barbecue restaurants?
A slab of anything.

CHAPTER 4

WHAT'S THE DIFFERENCE?

What's the difference between a fruit crop and a Note Block?
One is Melon-y, and the other plays a melody.

■

What's the difference between Antarctica and the Ice Plains?
One is a no man's land, and the other is a snowman's land.

■

What's the difference between a bully and Obsidian?
One is the toughest guy on the block and the other is the toughest Block on a guy.

■

What's the difference between school and *Minecraft*?
One is boring, and the other is ore-ing.

What's the difference between an Enderman and a house?
One hates stares and the other has stairs.

What's the difference between a Cow and a Chicken?
One drops leathers and the other drops feathers.

■

What's the difference between a Tree and an Evoker?
The bite is worse than the bark!

What's the difference between a Horse and a Skeleton?
One was a pony, and the other is quite bony.

What's the difference between a tamed Ocelot and a Shulker?
One likes to purr and the other likes purpurs.

■

What's the difference between a Cow and a Creeper?
One moos and one moossssss.

What's the difference between a lighted block and a Vex?
One is a beacon and the other is beakin'.

■

What do Australia and the Nether have in common?
They're both Down Under!

■

Which weighs more, a ton of Redstone or a ton of Glowstone?
They *both* weigh a ton.

■

How is an Enderman like an oyster?
It's hard to get them to give up their Pearls.

■

What do a Dog's tail and a minecart have in common?
One's a waggin' and the other's a wagon.

■

What do Parrots and parents have in common?
They don't like you playing too much *Minecraft*!

What's the difference between a Witch's potion, and some Obsidian?

One is a bracken brew and the other is black and blue.

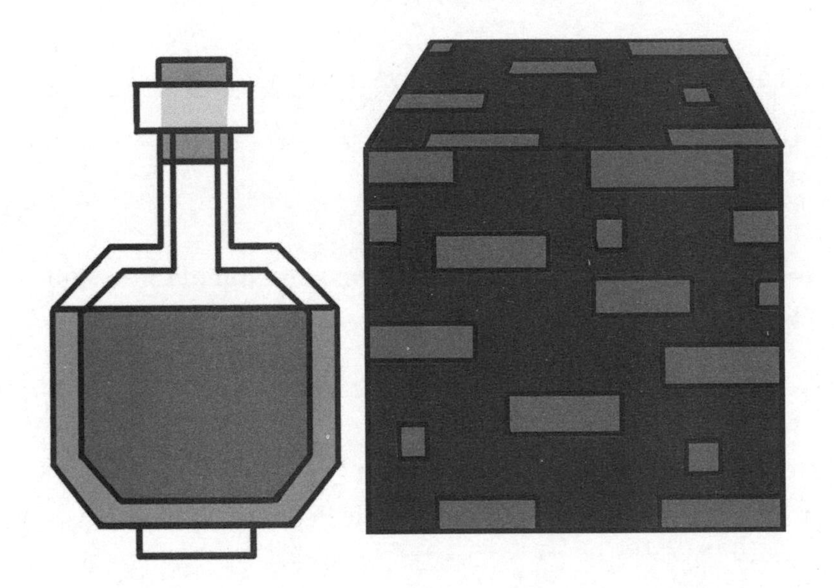

CHAPTER 5

BIOMES AND OTHER HOMES

What state would Minecrafters like to visit?
Minersota.

■

In what Colorado city could a Minecrafter live?
Boulder.

■

What California area would appeal to Steve?
Pebble Beach.

■

What Georgia city sounds like a biome?
Savannah.

What Arizona city sounds like a biome?
Mesa.

■

What mountain range sounds the most *Minecraft*-y?
The Rocky Mountains.

■

This place where four states meet sounds like a *Minecraft* feature.
Four Corners.

■

This Nordic country sounds like a biome.
Iceland.

■

This large island also sounds like it could be a biome.
Greenland.

■

Why did the Minecrafter enjoy *The Wizard of Oz*?
Because of the Emerald City.

Which Pennsylvania city sounds like it's full of mines?
Pittsburgh.

■

This is the capital of Arkansas, and could also be a *Minecraft* thing.
Little Rock.

■

Minecrafters would love this Illinois city.
Rockford.

■

This west coast state is home to lots of Minecrafters.
Ore-gon.

■

This city in Michigan isn't *entirely* made of ore.
Flint.

■

Is this Southwestern state a *Minecraft* paradise?
Ore-izona.

This city in Texas has definitely got to be a biome.
Grand Prairie.

■

This city in Kansas sounds like it came straight out of *Minecraft*.
Overland Park.

■

If the major Texas city of San Antonio was located in *Minecraft,* it would be called . . .
Sand-and-Stony-O.

■

Is this an island, or an 8-bit item?
Cube-a.

■

This Southwestern state might be full of trees.
Oak-lahoma.

■

This California town might also have a lot of Wood ready to go.
Oak-land.

This famous city in Louisiana might have lots of rocks and gems.
New Ore-leans.

■

Minecrafters looking for a vacation might visit this place in Mexico.
Rockapulco.

■

What did the Canadian Minecrafter call the biome they'd never seen?
Newfoundland.

■

What's the best thing to do in the Ice Biome?
Chill.

■

Why is the Ocean Biome blue?
Because it's under the weather.

How did the Skeleton get to a grassy biome?
He took an arrow-plane.

Where do Ghasts get their strength?
At the Ghast station.

Where do Witches Spawn?
In Wichita.

Where do Blazes spawn?
In Phoenix.

Which biome has the worst popsicles?
The Ice Plains.

■

Why does Steve look out the window in the morning?
Because he couldn't see through the wall.

■

What happened to the Minecrafter's computer when he went to the Ice Biome?
It froze.

■

Why didn't Steve want to explore the ocean?
There was something fishy about it.

■

Which is the best biome to take a nap?
The For-rest.

■

How do you play *Minecraft* in the sky?
With an air-craft.

How do you play *Minecraft* in the ocean?
With a water-craft.

■

It has a mouth but can't eat. What is it?
A river!

■

What has a bed but doesn't sleep?
A river.

■

What's the most valuable part of a river?
The banks.

■

What do you call an Enderman in the Taiga?
Lost!

■

What should you do if you find gravel cliffs in the Nether?
Stay away from them!

What do you call a room with no windows or doors?
A Mushroom!

Why did Steve fly to a remote biome?
Because it was too far to walk.

■

Where would you find an ocean liner in *Minecraft*?
In the desert—because sand lines the ocean.

When Steve was broke he went to the desert. Why?
To look for sand dollars.

■

What's the capital of *Minecraft*?
The M!

■

Why didn't Steve starve in the Desert?
Because of all the sand . . . which is there.

■

What did Steve say when he fell down the narrow shaft?
"I'm all in!"

■

Which is the funniest biome?
Any of the Hills. They're hill-arious!

■

It's really cold in the Icy Biome.
Snow joke. It's just really cold there.

Where would you go for fun in the sun, except there isn't much sun so it's not much fun?
Cold Beach.

■

Why are *Minecraft* caves so dark?
Because they block out the light!

■

Where will you always find a Minecrafter?
Hanging around on corners.

■

What's the problem with deep *Minecraft* caves?
They drive you batty.

■

Where do Minecrafters get their taxes done?
H&R Block.

■

What could you call a Villager's hut?
A panic room.

This is Steve's favorite kind of dancing.
Square dancing.

■

Why did Steve go to bed?
Because the bed wouldn't go to him.

■

What cannot be broken, yet can kill you before you know it?
The Void.

CHAPTER 6

MORE WHAT AM I?

Are you a fun guy? Do you know Fun Gus? This biome may be just right for you! What am I?
Mushroom Island.

■

Sometimes I'm green, sometimes I'm yellow. But I'm never red, so I'm not a traffic light. What am I?
An Experience Orb.

■

I plow and plow but never sow. What am I?
A Pig.

■

I make my lair out of string and catch my prey with a bite . . . or a sting. What am I?
A Spider.

I wear a coat in the winter and pants in the summer. What am I?
A Dog.

Alive without breath, cold as death.
Never thirsty, but always drinking.
What am I?
Silverfish.

■

I can swim or walk for miles.
I'm big with thick, white hair.
What am I?
A Polar Bear.

I always leaf and am there when things get punchy. What am I?
A Tree.

■

I am a hunk. Or a slice. Or a chunk. Or a piece.
What am I?
A Slab.

■

I am *not* a fan of water. What am I?
Enderman, Snowman, Blaze, Slime, Magma Cube . . .

■

No armor, enchantment or weapon can stop me. The cure is so simple. What am I?
Hunger.

■

A world of green contains a world of red, spotted with black and white freckles. What am I?
A Watermelon.

I am highly sought after by every man. And yet I have no worth or special purpose. What am I?
Dragon egg.

■

I make color, but I am gray. What am I?
Squid.

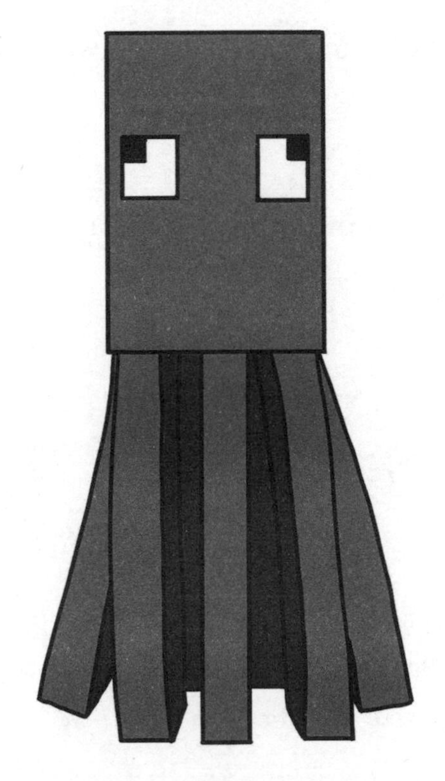

Rain, rain, go away, come back another day, says I. What am I?
A Husk.

■

Why hadn't Steve slept in days?
Because he sleeps nights.

■

What runs around a field but doesn't move?
A fence!

■

What changes on its own every seven days, but only for ten seconds when you try to change it?
The weather.

■

What falls, but never breaks? What breaks, but never falls?
Day and night.

■

Steve built a one-story house. There were all kinds of rooms, and a tower, and hundreds of torches. Where did he put the stairs?
Nowhere, because it was a one-story house!

What made Alex suddenly stand still, completely frozen where she stood?
The pause button!

■

What are the happiest flowers in *Minecraft*?
Dandy-lions.

■

The red house is made of red bricks.
The blue house is made of blue bricks.
What is the greenhouse made of?
Glass!

■

How do you make a goldfish age?
Take out the "g."

■

I used to be on paper, now I'm totally electronic. And I can always show you the right way. What am I?
A map.

I see you, but do not speak, only wave. What am I?
The Ocean.

■

Only after you grab this tool can you take your pick. What am I?
A Pickaxe.

■

You can fight or hunt with words, so long as you rearrange me first. What am I?
Sword. (Move the "s" on "words" to the front of "word," and you get "sword"!)

■

I am a transparent tool, but I am not a Glass Bottle. What am I?
Shears.

■

I'm usually the sign that things are over, but in *Minecraft* I'm just the beginning. What am I?
The End.

We're part of a neighborhood or a city, but you'll find us in even the most empty space in *Minecraft*. What are we?
Blocks!

■

I help you live by *not* living. What am I?
An animal in Minecraft.

■

I may look like a Tree, but I am not covered in leaves. What am I?
A Creeper.

■

Enter me, the time is three. Exit me, the time is . . . three?! What am I?
The Nether.

■

I am alive, but I am dead. How can this be? What happened to me?
It's a Zombie.

I am alive, but I am dead. You never "sausage" a sight!
Zombie Pigman.

■

In trying to vanquish you, I vanquish myself. It's so frustrating I could explode! What am I?
A Creeper.

■

I am full of Trees, but I am not the Forest. What am I?
The Jungle.

■

If you shout out, "Hey, you," we will come even though you didn't call us. Who are we?
A Horse and a Sheep. (We thought you said "hay" and "ewe.")

■

With just a small addition, a Minecrafter could eat me. What am I?
Desert. (Desert + s = dessert.)

Alone we are cold, but when we get together we make sparks fly! What are we?

Flint and Steel.

■

I come from the Void . . . and "avoid" me is what you ought to do. What am I?

Enderman.

■

I am a weapon, but you cannot build me or find me, for you already have me. What am I?

Fists.

■

I provide protection from the Void, but you cannot "rest" on me. What am I?

Bedrock.

■

I am a fire-man . . . but I don't put out fires. What am I?

Blaze.

I am very useful, but can also be a real "pane." What am I?
A glass block.

■

I am very hard to find, and if a friend has me you'll be green with envy—but not as green as me. What am I?
An emerald block.

■

We're very good at spelling, but you won't find us in any school or spelling bee. What are we?
Witches.

■

We're useless alone, and our names even rhyme. We just belong together. What are we?
Bow and arrow.

■

We don't have any "body." No bones about it. What are we?
Skeletons.

In the real world, you'd find us on the back of a horse, but in *Minecraft* we ride upon monsters, of course. What are we?
Spider Jockeys.

We'll show you what "fun guys" we can be . . . if you give us plenty of "room." What are we?
Mushrooms.

Feed me lava or milk. I can handle either! What am I?
A Bucket.

■

Are we the most valuable fish in *Minecraft*? Sure, because there are no goldfish in *Minecraft*! What are we?
Silverfish.

■

I am the only thing separating your Overwold from the darkness of the Void. What am I?
Bedrock.

■

I am the only thing that can destroy Bedrock. What am I?
Nothing!

■

Grass won't grow on me, but other plants can. What am I?
Podzol.

When you destroy me, I fall to pieces. Still, you cannot rebuild me. What am I?
Glass.

■

Once I die, my secret becomes known to you. What am I?
Enderdragon.

■

I am known to be harmless, yet, I am not defenseless. What am I?
Pigman.

■

Souls are trapped in me, and can never get out. What am I?
Soul Sand.

■

The most ruthless and the most rare. You may think I'm harmless, but you're off by just a hare.
What am I?
Killer Bunny.

CHAPTER 7

TOOLING AROUND

Animals drop things. What does Steve drop?
Anvils.

■

What do cutting tools say when they share a drink?
"Shears!"

■

What kind of fish do Minecrafters eat?
Smelt.

■

Alex: Who left all this stone in the furnace?
Steve: Whoever smelt it, dealt it!

Why should you worry about crafters who use anvils?
Because they're anvillains!

■

What did Steve say to the Torch?
"You light up my life!"

Why did Steve have to go back home for his tools?
Because he got benched.

Why didn't Steve's minecart work?
Because it was tired.

■

Was the Torch happy when it was extinguished?
Yes, it was de-lighted!

■

What happened to Steve's house when he installed a torch?
It became a light-house!

■

Why couldn't Steve stop fishing?
Once he started, he got hooked.

■

What's the fastest tool in *Minecraft*?
The clocks—they're always running.

■

How do you make a stool in *Minecraft*?
Just sit on a Mushroom—it's a toadstool!

What kind of ruler is the difference between life and death?
A health meter.

■

Why was the Torch uptight?
Because it needed to lighten up.

■

Where do Minecrafters go for extra cash?
The spawn shop.

■

Why was Steve mad at a Tree?
He had an Axe to grind.

■

Why did the Minecrafter run away with a light source?
Because it was a Torch-and-go situation.

■

Why was the Redstone sad?
It was tired of getting picked on.

Where do tools stay when they're on vacation?
At a hoe-tel.

■

Do hippies like *Minecraft*?
Yeah, mine, they totally dig it.

■

What happened when Steve got way too deep underground?
He could feel his cart pounding.

■

What did one Torch say to the other Torch?
"Do you wanna go out tonight?"

■

Why didn't Steve bother with the train tracks?
He just didn't have the cart.

■

How do you ask a question in *Minecraft*?
You send a quarry.

What do you call a torch on the ceiling?
A high light.

■

This tool is all-encompassing but it only does one thing. What is it?
A compass.

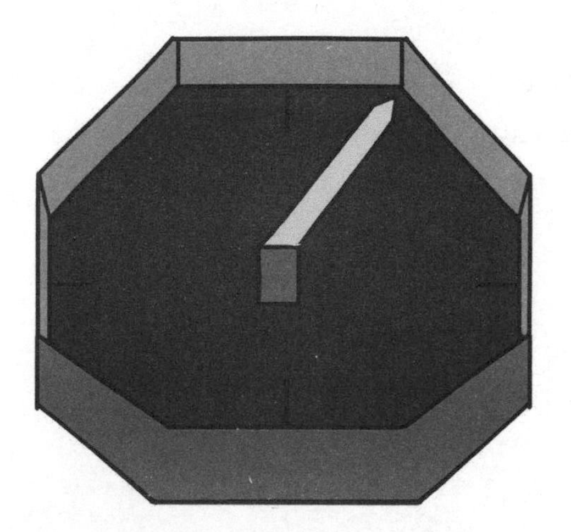

What did one Sword say to other Sword?
"You're looking sharp!"

■

How do Minecrafters send letters?
With an axe machine.

If it took eight men ten hours to build a wall, how long would it take four men to build it?
No time at all, since the wall is already built!

■

What bow has no arrows?
A rainbow!

■

How do you learn more about *Minecraft* tools?
Axe questions!

■

What do you call a Lever that doesn't work?
A severed Lever.

■

Why did Steve swallow his own Clock at sundown?
He needed a night watchman.

■

Where do young Minecrafters go before they become miners?
To tool!

Why did Steve chop down a Tree?
It was knotty.

■

What would you call the history of a minecart?
An auto-biography.

■

After punching trees, why did Steve grab a clock?
Because time heals all wounds.

■

Where does a Minecrafter go to get their shoes repaired?
A cobbler.

■

What did Alex say when she offered Steve a bunch of Axes?
"Take your pick!"

■

What did Steve do when he felt ill?
He built a dock-tor.

Steve punched down a tree and then asked it how it felt. How did the tree respond?

It didn't—it was stumped.

What do you call a boat in *Minecraft*?

A *Minecraft* Raft.

Why do Shears make good cart drivers?
They know all the shortcuts!

■

How did Steve and Alex decide who got to mine first?
They played Stone, Paper, Shears!

■

Why did Steve go to the dentist?
For an extraction.

■

How do Minecrafters party?
They raise the roof!

■

Why did nosey Steve build such a bad roof?
He kept eavesdropping.

■

What did Alex do when Steve gave her a diamond ring?
She mined obsidian with it.

Why did Steve give his Cow a hammer at night time?
It was time for it to hit the hay!

■

Where did Steve find a helping hand?
At the end of his arm.

■

What did Steve say as he dug into a giant shaft?
"Let's get to the bottom of this!"

■

What did Steve do when his life meter was low and he thought he was dying?
He built a living room.

■

Why did Steve build a place for horses?
He wanted something stable in his life.

■

Why did Steve build a suit of Armor?
Because he needed a knight gown.

Why did Santa start playing *Minecraft*?
To get a hoe-hoe-hoe.

■

What do you call a miner without an eye?
A mner.

■

Why couldn't Steve lift his treasure?
He had Chest pains.

■

What's the problem with finding diamonds near lava?
You get rich or die trying.

■

Why did Steve win a debate with a Diamond Sword?
He had a good point.

■

Why are Minecrafters so selfish?
Because everything is always "mine, mine, mine!"

How do Minecrafters pick their noses?
With a Pickaxe!

■

What kind of jokes do Minecrafters like best?
Swordplay.

■

What can you put in stone to make it lighter?
A hole.

■

What do you get when you cross TNT and Ice?
Chaos!

■

What kind of car would the female protagonist of *Minecraft* drive?
Alex's.

What kind of dinosaurs would you find in *Minecraft*?
Dino-mite.

■

What's the very first thing you see in *Minecraft*?
M!

CHAPTER 8

PASSIVE MOBS AND CUDDLY CREATURES

Why can't you complain when you haven't spawned any Cows?
Because you've got no beef!

■

Where do all the Cows in *Minecraft* go when they're not on screen?
The mooooovies.

■

Why are Squid so imposing?
Because they're well-armed!

■

How can you tell if a Squid likes you?
He'll ink at you!

How do Snow Golems get around?
Via icicle.

■

How do you make a Squid laugh?
With ten-tickles!

■

What would you call a dumb Squid?
A squidiot.

■

What did the Squid say when he dropped an item?
"Just squidding!"

■

What happened when the Squid found some gold?
Inky ingots!

■

What do you call an Snow Golem with a tool?
An ice-sickle

How does a Golem get bigger?
By pumping Iron!

How do Sheep love to waste time?
By watching Ewe-Tube.

■

What do you call a resident of a chilly biome?
You call em' Golems!

How does a Snow Golem find its home biome?
He finds it to be brrrr-fect!

■

A bunch of Cows wandered away from Farmland.
It was an udder catastrophe.

■

What happens when you cross a Snow Golem with an Iron Golem?
You get a puddle.

■

What's another way to make a Water Block?
Take a Snow Golem to the Desert.

■

What did the Snow Golem's mom call him?
Her little pumpkinhead!

■

Where do all the Mules go when you don't need them?
To the Mule-seum.

Can a Polar Bear build a *Minecraft* house?
Sure, igloos it together.

■

How do you call a Polar Bear wearing earmuffs?
You don't—he can't hear you!

■

What do you call a Cow that doesn't do anything?
A Milk Dud!

■

How do you communicate with Fish?
Drop them a line.

■

What is leather used for most in *Minecraft*?
Holding the Cows together!

■

Are Cows the best animal in *Minecraft*?
Whatever, it's a moooot point.

What happened when the Ocelot wandered onto the beach biome?
Sandy Claws!

■

What do you get when you cross an Evoker with an Snow Golem?
Frostbite.

■

When a Rabbit drops a Rabbit's foot, it's lucky for all but who?
The Rabbit!

■

What kind of shows do NPCs like?
Talk shows.

■

How do you make fir trees in *Minecraft*?
Put a rabbit in a tree.

Did you hear about the Rabbit that didn't notice the garden of free food?
It's like he didn't carrot all!

■

How do you make a hedgehog in *Minecraft*?
Throw a Pig into some hedges.

■

Where can you find a horse in *Minecraft*?
In their neigh-borhood.

■

Why won't Bats take sides in an argument?
They prefer to stay neutral.

■

How do you summon your horse?
"Hay!"

■

What did the Snow Golem say to the Torch?
"I melt when I'm around you!"

Where in *Minecraft* would you shear a sheep?
At the baa-baa shop.

■

What happens if you cross a Chicken with some Ore?
You get a featherweight boxer.

■

Do all the sheep in *Minecraft* look the same?
Yep—they're ewe-niform.

■

Why do white sheep eat more grass than dyed sheep?
Because there are more of them!

■

What do you get when you cross a Chicken with a Clock?
A cluck.

■

What do you get when you cross a Chicken with TNT?
Cock-a-doodle-boom!

What kind of dogs do Minecrafters like best?
Boxers.

■

What letter do you get when you've got two sheep?
W (Double-ewe).

■

Why is it nice to encounter rabbits?
Because they're so hoppy!

■

Cow #1: Did you know all cows in *Minecraft* are female?
Cow #2: Really?
Cow #1: Yep, no bull!

■

Why was the Chicken happy?
Everything was egg-cellent.

■

Why are Cows unreliable?
They're just so grazy!

How do you catch a unique Rabbit?
Unique up on him.

■

What did the sheep say after trying to eat a cactus?
Accidents Wool happen!

■

What does a Chicken drop after it eats Iron?
Chicken nuggets.

■

What do you call a boat full of Sheep with Swords?
A battlesheep!

■

What do Snow Golems clean with?
A brr-oom!

■

Why did Steve build a Chicken coop with only two doors?
Because if it had four doors, it would've been a sedan!

What do you get when a Chicken eats a bunch of ore?
A brick-layer!

■

Alex's shelter was chicken-proof.
Yep, it was im-peckable.

■

What do you call a sleeping Cow?
A bull-dozer.

What can't add, but can definitely multiply?
Rabbits.

■

Why did the Ocelot go to the cleaners?
To remove its spots.

■

Where do Ocelots shop?
Cat-alogs.

■

Why are the Cows in *Minecraft* so happy?
Because every day is a moo day.

■

What's the loudest animal in *Minecraft*?
The blah blah black Sheep.

■

What kind of teeth live in the coldest biomes?
Molar bears.

A horse is tied to a fifteen-foot rope and there is a bale of hay twenty feet away. The horse, however, is still able to eat from the hay. How is this possible?
The rope wasn't tied to anything!

■

Dogs have fleas. What do Sheep have?
Fleece.

■

What did the Dog say when he sat on a rough plank?
Rough!

■

Can Ocelots sing?
Sure, they're very mewsical.

■

When's the best time of day to spawn Cows?
In the moooonlight.

■

Why are Bats hard to be around?
Because they have Bat breath.

Why was the Rabbit unhappy?
It was having a bad hare day.

Why can't Ocelots play Hide-and-Seek?
They're always spotted.

■

What do you call a Chicken in the Tundra?
A brrrrrd!

How do you make a porcupine in *Minecraft*?
Cross a pig with a tree. Get it?

■

What animal can jump higher than the highest building you can build in *Minecraft*?
Any or all of them—buildings can't jump!

■

What kind of Chicken drops blue feathers?
A sad one.

■

What happened to the Sheep that stepped on a flower?
It dyed.

■

Did you hear about the mean *Minecraft* sheep?
It was a real Wooly Bully.

■

Why are Chickens so cool?
Because they wear feather jackets.

Why do Squid like salt water?

Because pepper makes them sneeze.

■

What's Herobrine's favorite kind of music?

Rock and troll!

CHAPTER 9

SWIFTLY, ALEX!

"I just love putting up the supports for my structure!" Alex beamed.

■

"There are Chickens in my yard!" clucked Alex cockily.

"This Cow never runs out of milk," Alex uttered continuously.

■

"Creepers are always showing up," said Alex incidentally.

■

"I've got to fix the cart," said Alex mechanically.

■

"I wish it was still night time," Alex mourned.

■

"I need to sleep," said Alex, nodding.

■

"I have more windows than I need," said Alex painfully.

■

"I wouldn't work Glass blocks with my hands," said Alex painstakingly.

■

"I've just cut myself with a Pickaxe!" said Alex pointedly.

"The door is over there," Alex pointed out.

■

"My sword is dull," said Alex pointlessly.

"All my flowers died," said Alex witheringly.

■

"Stop that horse!" cried Alex with woe.

"Let's go tame one," said Alex wolfishly.

■

"This river is rough," said Alex rapidly.

■

"There's that Enderman again!" Alex recited.

■

"I'm measuring for my shelter again," Alex remarked.

■

"I'm not going to build beyond this point," Alex ruled.

■

"Can I use this Sword yet?" Alex cut in sharply.

■

"I'm very strong!" said Alex soberly.

■

"Get to the back of the boat," said Alex sternly.

■

"This shaft is infested," said Alex trenchantly.

"This isn't a real Emerald," said Alex stonily.

"I've brought back the Cart I borrowed," said Alex truculently.

■

"I don't think I'll eat any Fish today," said Alex unerringly.

■

"I flew from one biome to the other," said Alex, visibly moved.

■

"Every second in *Minecraft* feels like it lasts for seven days," said Alex in a moment of weakness.

CHAPTER 10

YOU KNOW YOU'RE A MINECRAFTER IF . . .

The craft store is not what you were expecting.

■

You've asked your parents how babies spawn.

■

When you played with blocks as a toddler, you built a fully immersive world filled with creatures.

■

You're jealous of the cat for getting to play in a literal sandbox.

■

Your favorite rapper is Ice Cube.

You'd rather have Desert than dessert.

■

You watch *The Flintstones* just for the bedrock.

■

You don't build snowmen, you build golems.

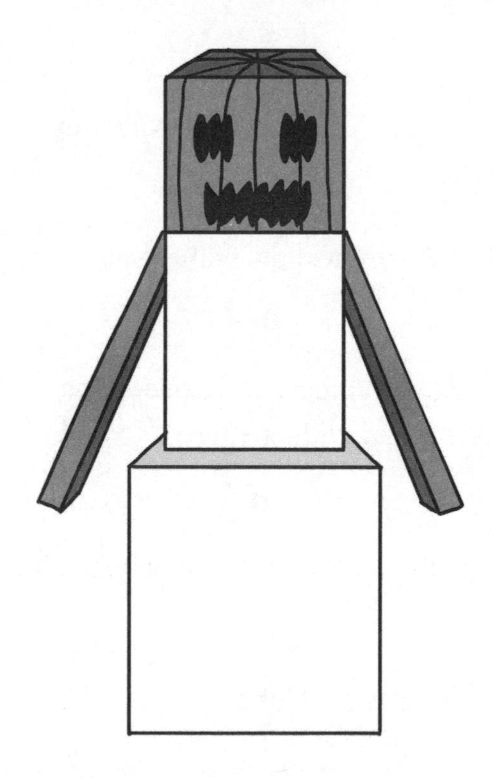

You call your pen an ink sac.

■

You're surprised when your real-life wooden pickaxe is useless.

■

You think *Bob the Builder* could work a little faster.

■

You're disappointed that "heart of gold" is only an expression.

■

You've tried to build a wall out of walnuts.

■

You think Notch should be on Mount Rushmore.

■

You've offered to cut down the family Christmas tree. With your hands.

■

You've suggested that your school go to a "block schedule."

A game of Jenga with you takes hours.

You'll play a dice game, but only so you can stack the dice.

■

When you go to a national monument, you're on the lookout for Guardians.

■

You assume anybody named Johnny is a Vindicator.

You can't listen to music with horns because you think it means a Vex is nearby.

■

You want to study geology in college.

■

You turn down the chance to go on a treasure hunt to stay home and play *Minecraft*.

■

You don't find the Great Wall of China to be particularly impressive.

■

You keep getting in trouble for putting things in the furnace.

■

When someone asks for a glass of water, you give them some sand and point them to the oven.

All you want to do at the beach is make sand castles.

You prefer all surfaces to be stained.

■

Whenever you hear counting, you duck because you think TNT is about to explode.

■

You call all boys "Steve" and all girls "Alex."

CHAPTER 11

KNOCK-KNOCK . . .

Knock-knock . . .
Who's there?
Wood.
Wood who?
Wood you please open the door?

■

Knock-knock . . .
Who's there?
Wither.
Wither who?
I'm coming in, Wither you like it or not!

■

Knock-knock . . .
Who's there?
Everest.
Everest who?
Everest, or is it just build, build, build?

■

Knock-knock . . .
Who's there?
Endermite.
Endermite who?
Open the door, Endermite not kill you!

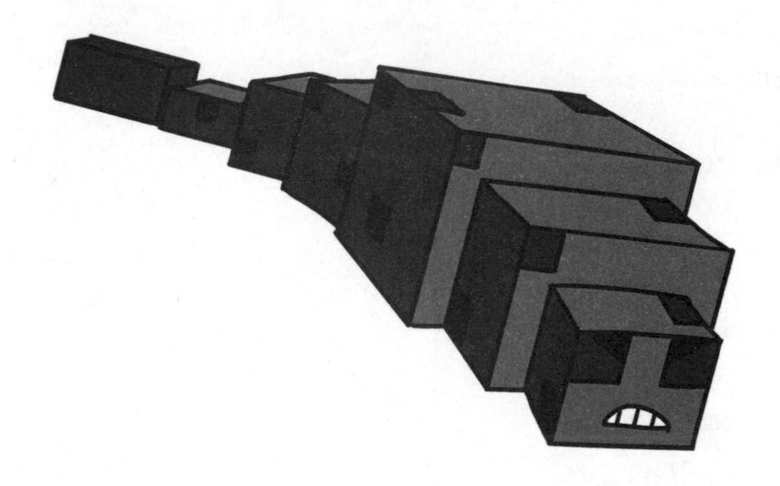

Knock-knock . . .
Who's there?
Juicy.
Juicy who?
Juicy any Creepers around?

■

Knock-knock . . .
Who's there?
Donut.
Donut who?
Donut open the door—there are Hostiles around!

■

Knock-knock . . .
Who's there?
Peas.
Peas who?
Peas come outside and help me dig!

■

Knock-knock . . .
Who's there?
Alex.
Alex who?
Alex plain when you open the door!

■

Knock-knock . . .
Who's there?
Alex.
Alex who?
Hey, Alex the questions!

■

Knock-knock . . .
Who's there?
Macon.
Macon who?
Stand back, I'm Macon my own way in!

■

Knock-knock . . .
Who's there?
Megan.
Megan who?
Megan stuff in *Minecraft* is the best!

■

Knock-knock . . .
Who's there?
Zany.
Zany who?
Zany body wanna go for a dig?

■

Knock-knock . . .
Who's there?
Norway.
Norway who?
Norway I'm staying out here with all these Zombies and Skeletons!

■

Knock-knock . . .
Who's there?
Allison.
Allison who?
Allison for hissing, and if I hear it, can I come in?

■

Knock-knock . . .
Who's there?
Gwen.
Gwen who?
Gwen do you think you want to play *Minecraft*?

■

Knock-knock . . .
Who's there?
Interrupting Blaze.
Interruping Bla—
Sizzle . . .

Knock-knock . . .
Who's there?
Interrupting Ghast.
Interrupting Gha—
Chirp-chirp!

■

Knock-knock . . .
Who's there?
Boat.
Boat who?
Boat time you got out here and mined!

■

Knock-knock . . .
Who's there?
Seed.
Seed who?
Seeds spawn!

■

Knock-knock . . .
Who's there?
Iguana.
Iguana who?
Iguana come in and play *Minecraft*!

■

Knock-knock . . .
Who's there?
Raven.
Raven who?
I've been raven about *Minecraft* to all my friends!

■

Knock-knock . . .
Who's there?
Al.
Al who?
Al give you some Ore if you let me in!

■

Knock-knock . . .
Who's there?
Denise.
Denise who?
Denise hurt from where the Skeleton shot me!

■

Knock-knock . . .
Who's there?
Canoe.
Canoe who?
Canoe give me some gems?

■

Knock-knock . . .
Who's there?
Iva.
Iva who?
Iva sore hand from punching trees!

■

Knock-knock . . .
Who's there?
Dishes.
Dishes who?
Dissssshes a Creeper. *BOOM!*

■

Knock-knock . . .
Who's there?
Husk.
Husk who?
Bless you!

■

Knock-knock . . .
Who's there?
Biome.
Biome who?
Why would I Biome when I can build one?

■

Knock-knock . . .
Who's there?
Guardian.
Guardian who?
Guardian your shelter, there are laser-shooting fish out here!

■

Knock-knock . . .
Who's there?
Fish.
Fish who?
Fish who shoot lasers!

■

Knock-knock . . .
Who's there?
Geno.
Geno who?
Geno any good *Minecraft* tips?

■

Knock-knock . . .

Who's there?

Barry.

Barry who?

Barry the treasure before anyone can steal it!

■

Knock-knock . . .

Who's there?

Cow.

Cow who?

Cowhide!

■

Knock-knock . . .

Who's there?

Sadie.

Sadie who?

Sadie air is hot in this Desert!

■

Knock-knock . . .
Who's there?
Kenya.
Kenya who?
I've fallen in a shaft, Kenya help me?

■

Knock-knock . . .
Who's there?
Broken Sword.
Broken Sword who?
Ah, it's pointless.

■

Knock-knock . . .
Who's there?
Ivan.
Ivan who?
Ivan working hard on my shelter!

■

Knock-knock . . .
Who's there?
Ivana.
Ivana who?
Ivana get you, because this is a Wither!

■

Knock-knock . . .
Who's there?
Wanda.
Wanda who?
Wanda where I left my tools.

■

Knock-knock . . .
Who's there?
Wooden Axe.
Wooden Axe who?
Wooden Axe me twice next time, wood you?

■

Knock-knock . . .
Who's there?
Witch.
Witch who?
Witch you would let me in!

■

Knock-knock . . .
Who's there?
Hurd.
Hurd who?
I Hurd my hand punching trees and it hurts to knock!

■

Knock-knock . . .
Who's there?
Coal Mine.
Coal Mine who?
Coal mines are just waiting for us to dig in!

■

Knock-knock . . .
Who's there?
May.
May who?
May I borrow a Torch, please?

■

Knock-knock . . .
Who's there?
Coal.
Coal who?
It's so Coal out here!

■

Knock-knock . . .
Who's there?
Ewe.
Ewe who?
Ewe've made your bed, now Sheep in it.

■

Knock-knock . . .
Who's there?
Havana.
Havana who?
Havana wonderful time playing *Minecraft*?

■

Knock-knock . . .
Who's there?
Olive.
Olive who?
Olive playing *Minecraft*!

■

Knock-knock . . .
Who's there?
Huron.
Huron who?
Huron the spot I wanted to build!

■

Knock-knock . . .
Who's there?
Thumping.
Thumping who?
Thumping just stole your Emeralds!

■

Knock-knock . . .
Who's there?
Scold.
Scold who?
Scold out here in the Ice Biome!

■

Knock-knock . . .
Who's there?
Philip.
Philip my chest with emeralds, please!

■

Knock-knock . . .
Who's there?
Tamara.
Tamara who?
Tamara we'll build something new together!

■

Knock-knock . . .
Who's there?
Aardvark.
Aardvark who?
Aardvark a million miles to play *Minecraft*!

■

Knock-knock . . .
Who's there?
Canoe.
Canoe who?
Canoe lend me some tools?

■

Knock-knock . . .
Who's there?
Formosa.
Formosa who?
Formosa the summer I played *Minecraft*.

■

Knock-knock . . .
Who's there?
Disguise.
Disguise who?
Disguise a big fan of *Minecraft*!

■

Knock-knock . . .
Who's there?
Jamaica.
Jamaica who?
Jamaica huge tower yet?

■

Knock-knock . . .
Who's there?
Jim.
Jim who?
Jim mind if I come in and play *Minecraft?*

■

Knock-knock . . .
Who's there?
Handsome.
Handsome who?
Handsome of those Emeralds to me!

■

Knock-knock . . .
Who's there?
Doug.
Doug who?
I Doug deep and still couldn't find any Emeralds!

■

Knock-knock . . .
Who's there?
House.
House who?
House is great, you build it yourself?

■

Knock-knock . . .
Who's there?
Wayne.
Wayne who?
The Wayne is coming down, let me in!

■

Knock-knock . . .
Who's there?
Guitar.
Guitar who?
Let's guitar Pickaxes and go find some Diamonds!

■

Knock-knock . . .
Who's there?
Stew.
Stew who?
Stew you want me to make you a Mushroom Stew?

■

Knock-knock . . .
Who's there?
Water.
Water who?
Water Blocks!

■

Knock-knock . . .
Who's there?
Ida.
Ida who?
Ida called first, but there are no phones in *Minecraft*!

■

Knock-knock . . .
Who's there?
Stan.
Stan who?
Stan back, I'm going to break that Pressure Plate!

■

Knock-knock . . .
Who's there?
Interrupting Zombie.
Interrupting Zombie who?
Braaaains!

Knock-knock . . .
Who's there?
Weird.
Weird who?
Weird you hide the Diamonds?

■

Knock-knock . . .
Who's there?
Dishes.
Dishes who?
Dishes Alex, open up!

■

Knock-knock . . .
Who's there?
Rock
Rock who?
"Rock a bye baby in the treetop . . . "

■

Knock-knock . . .
Who's there?
Zombies.
Zombies who?
Zombies make honey, others don't.

■

Knock-knock . . .
Who's there?
Alpaca.
Alpaca who?
Alpaca chest full of Emeralds for you!

■

Knock-knock . . .
Who's there?
Clara.
Clara who?
Clara space and let's build something new!

■

Knock-knock . . .
Who's there?
Anita.
Anita who?
Anita borrow a Pickaxe!

■

Knock-knock . . .
Who's there?
Pig.
Pig who?
Pig up all your Emeralds or you're going to lose them!

■

Knock-knock . . .
Who's there?
Xavier.
Xavier who?
Xavier self—there are hostiles everywhere!

■

Knock-knock . . .
Who's there?
Needle.
Needle who?
Needle light? Get a Torch!

■

Knock-knock . . .
Who's there?
Crash!
Oh no, I played on hard mode!

■

Knock-knock . . .
Who's there?
Ocelot.
Ocelot who?
You Ocelot of questions!

CHAPTER 12

JUST PLAIN DUMB

Where does Steve buy his blue pants?
At the blue pants store.

■

How does a miner go to the bathroom in an Enderportal?
In a portal-potty.

■

This is the coldest version of *Minecraft*.
Minedraft.

■

Where does soul sand grow?
Nether. You mind?

■

Why do cows have bells?
Their horns don't work.

Why was Steve so good at yoga?
Because he lived in the right Bi-ohm.

How you make a pincushion in *Minecraft*?
Run through a group of skeletons.

■

How can pigs fly?
Apply enough TNT.

■

Why is *Minecraft* made of blocks?
You can't build with circles.

How many tickles does it take to make a Squid laugh?
Ten-ticles.

■

What's the best way to catch a fish in *Minecraft*?
Have another player throw one at you.

■

How do you count your Cows?
With a cow-culator.

■

What kind of snake plays *Minecraft*?
A boa constructor.

■

Who built the first tunnel in *Minecraft*?
A worm, probably!

■

What did the farming Villager grow after he worked very hard?
Tired.

What in *Minecraft* is brown and sticky?
A stick.

■

What's the dirtiest thing in *Minecraft*?
Dirt.

■

What's the hardest thing in *Minecraft*?
The rocks.

■

What's the hardest mode in *Minecraft*?
Hard mode.

■

Why is *Minecraft* child's play?
Because all you have to do is play with blocks!

■

How do you bring about peace?
Play *Minecraft* on Peaceful Mode.

Why was Steve holding a carrot in his hand?
He must have eaten his Pickaxe for lunch.

■

How can you tell if a Cow is male or female?
If you're playing *Minecraft*, it's female.

■

What's the one thing about digging a hole in *Minecraft*?
It's so boring.

■

How do you stop a boat in *Minecraft*?
Sing "whoa whoa whoa, the boat . . . "

■

What do you get when you pound Ores together?
Rock music.

■

Why is Notch so cool?
Because he has millions of fans.

Steve wasn't always a confident miner, you know.
First he had to get a little boulder.

■

Which side of a Rabbit is the furriest?
The outside.

■

What did one Ore say to the other Ore?
Nothing. Ore doesn't talk.

■

How did they decide to add polar bears to *Minecraft*?
They took a North Poll.

■

What did one hay bale say to the other hay bale?
"Hay, bale!"

■

What did the Grass say to the Dirt?
"I've got you covered!"

What kind of trees grow on a miner's hands?
Palm trees!

■

What's a Tree's favorite drink?
Root beer.

■

What's a Tree's least favorite drink?
Punch!

■

Why is Grass so dangerous?
Because it's full of blades!

■

What is a Tree's least favorite month?
Sep-timber.

■

Where do you find an ocean without water?
On a map!

Is the world round or flat?
In *Minecraft*? Neither!

■

What did Steve say when he walked into a tower?
"Ouch!"

■

What in *Minecraft* gets bigger the more you take away from it?
A hole!

■

If a Tree had a watch and checked it, what would it say?
Tree o'clock!

■

What did the floor say to the ceiling?
"Stop looking at me!"

■

What did one Ice block say to another Ice block?
"You are so cool!"

Why did the Ice block strike up the conversation?
Because it was an ice thing to do.

■

What did Steve say when he fell into a mineshaft?
"Well, I guess I've hit rock bottom."

Why did Steve build a shelter on flat land?
Because it was flat.

■

What's the wettest thing in *Minecraft*?
A Water Block.

What's shinier than a diamond in *Minecraft*?
Two diamonds.

■

What do you call a Cow with seven legs?
A seven-legged Cow.

■

What did Steve say when he lost his Pickaxe?
"Where's my Pickaxe?"

■

Why did Steve put a Clock under his Workbench?
So he could have more time to build stuff.

■

Pretend you're surrounded by 100 skeletons and 200 creepers. What do you do?
Stop pretending!

■

When is a Minecart not a Minecart?
When it turns into a shaft.

Does a Skeleton Horse have any meat?
Neigh.

■

What in *Minecraft* is not so super-secret?
The super-secret settings.

■

What did Steve say to the Jack o' Lantern?
"Face it!"

■

What would you find on Farmland?
Farmers.

■

The only bars in *Minecraft*: iron bars.

■

What did Steve say when he saw a bunch of buildings?
"This is quite the development."

■

What shoe size does Steve wear?
Two square feet.

What should you do if you don't like the weather in *Minecraft*?
Change your altitude!

■

What's blue and turquoise and blue and turquoise and blue and turquoise and . . . ?
Steve falling down a hill.

■

How did Steve jump off a ladder without hurting himself?
He jumped off the bottom rung.

■

What happened when Steve listened to a Torch?
He burned his ear.

■

What will you find in every Village?
The town square.

■

What else will you find in the Village?
Villagers!

A man walked into an Iron Bar.
It hurt.

■

Why should you never let an Iron Golem hold your father?
Because they drop poppies!

■

Which *Minecraft* flower has a mouth?
The two-lips.

■

What's brown, messy, and everywhere in *Minecraft*?
Dirt.

■

What's one amazing thing you can do in the real world that you can't do in *Minecraft*?
Play *Minecraft!*

■

We'd tell you another shelter construction joke . . .
. . . but we're still working on it!

What big scary animal could you build in *Minecraft*?
A rockodile.

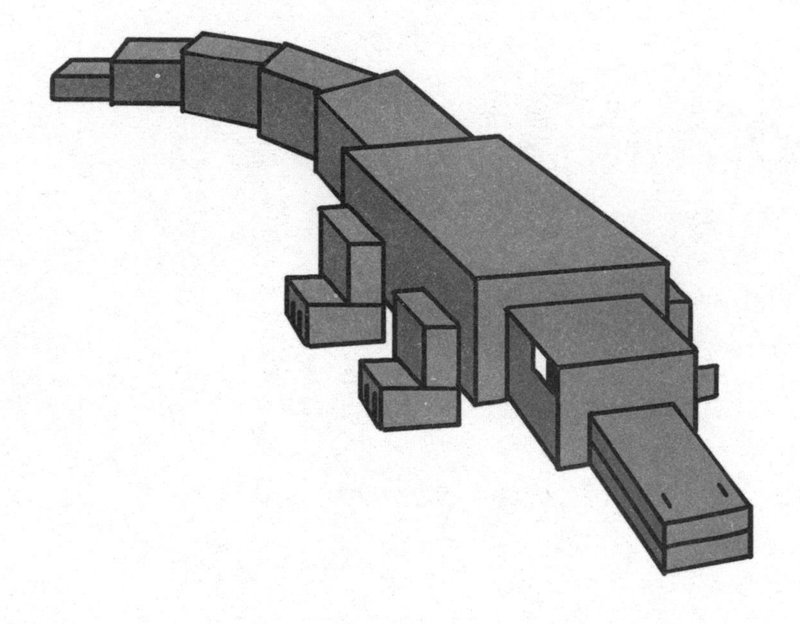

CHAPTER 13

MINECRAFT CRACKS AND WITTY WORDS OF WISDOM

Why is *Minecraft* always getting better? Because you can't "block" progress. Or then again, maybe you can . . .

■

The best part of *Minecraft*? The hole thing!

■

We'd tell you a story about how to beat *Minecraft,* but it might drag-on.

■

Is there more than one kind of dirt in *Minecraft*? Of coarse there is!

Sticks and stones may break your bones . . . and so will Zombies and Skeletons.

Ocelots are like potato chips. You can never have just one!

Geniuses enjoy playing *Minecraft.* They like mine games!

■

If life gives you lemons, well, you probably modded the game to include those lemons.

■

The place to go in *Minecraft* to get smarter is, of course, the master-mine.

■

Every slime story begins with "Once Upon A Slime."

Succeeding at this game is a simple act of mine over matter.

■

Minecrafters are often also photographers. They just like to see what develops.

■

Minecrafters wear boxers. Never briefs.

■

You play *Minecraft.* Your little brother or sister wants to play *Minecraft* so bad they might as well be playing *Whinecraft*!

■

Minecrafters don't get the blues—they get Lapiz Lazuli.

■

When you're in the sandy biomes, everything is Beachy keen!

■

Those who live in glass houses . . . would probably enjoy *Minecraft*.

Your *Minecraft* structures should win an award . . . for being outstanding in its field.

■

Hostiles might just be big fans of Steve and Alex. They're always "mobbing" them!

■

It's not hard to spot an Ocelot. They already come that way.

■

Playing *Minecraft* beats being a toddler. You don't have to choose between playing with blocks or playing with the sandbox. *Minecraft* is both!

■

When the moon comes up in the game, it's like a difference between night and day!

■

Minecraft: Before you can load your lode, you've got to let the code load!

Minecraft: You don't become a master right away. You build to it.

■

You can't get water from a stone . . . but you can put them next to each other in *Minecraft* and see what happens.

■

The path to a mine in *Minecraft* is merely the road to the lode!

■

Don't trust an Enderman. You can see right through them!

■

What's the great thing about the different types of *Minecraft* games? Whatever the mode, there's always a lode!

■

How is *Minecraft* better than ancient Rome? Because Rome wasn't built in a day, but you can build anything on *Minecraft* in minutes.

Minecrafters make great waiters and waitresses because they're familiar with servers.

■

The best and worst thing about *Minecraft*? The pitfalls.

■

Minecraft pigs are major blockheads.

■

If Christopher Columbus had been a Minecrafter, he might have set out to prove the world was square!

■

What do Notch and the Pilgrims have in common? Both made quite a life for themselves out of rocks—Notch with digitized ones, and the Pilgrims after they landed at Plymouth Rock.

■

Did you hear what happened to the Minecrafter who played for too long? She went wall-eyed!

"Three's company!" Sounds like something a Wither says!

■

Minecraft is the only place where getting stuck between a rock and a hard place is a good thing!

■

We'd tell you a joke about the *Minecraft* mountains . . . but you wouldn't get over it.

■

Calling someone a "square" is an insult to everyone but a Minecrafter. And Steve. And Alex.

■

"You're crushing it" is a compliment in real life. Not so much in *Minecraft!*

■

Minecraft is the best source of exercise there is! Why, there's walking, running, flying, swinging tools . . .

The tallest building you could ever build in *Minecraft*? Why, that would be the library, because it has so many stories!

■

With *Minecraft,* you can be there *and* be square!

■

Steve followed Alex to a new area, because they were friends till The End.

■

Alex and Steve survived The End . . . because everything always turns out alright in The End.

■

And finally, do you want to hear the world's longest *Minecraft* joke?

Here it comes.

Are you ready?

Okay.

Here it is.

Here is the world's longest *Minecraft* joke:

"The world's longest *Minecraft* joke."

AUTHOR BIOS

MICHELE C. HOLLOW is an award-winning writer who learned about Minecraft from her son, Jordon. She blogs at *Pet News and Views* and is the author of several children's books. She has absolutely no sense of humor, which her husband and son find ironic, but she doesn't get.

JORDON P. HOLLOW plays Minecraft every chance he gets. An avid reader, especially on the subject of Minecraft, Jordon loves mac 'n' cheese, grilled cheese, and Tastykake pies. He is a high school student.

STEVEN M. HOLLOW is an accomplished writer, actor, storyteller, puppeteer, and teaching artist. He began playing video games with the original introduction of Pong and plans to move on to other video games once he figures out how to move the paddles.

BRIAN BOONE is the author of *I Love Rock n' Roll (Except When I Hate It)* and many other books about everything from inventions to paper airplanes to magic to TV. He's written jokes for a lot of funny websites and he lives in Oregon with his family.